Y0-BUD-660

AMERICAN EDUCATION

Its Men

Ideas

and

Institutions

Advisory Editor

Lawrence A. Cremin
Frederick A. P. Barnard Professor of Education
Teachers College, Columbia University

The American College

A Criticism

Abraham Flexner

ARNO PRESS & THE NEW YORK TIMES
*New York * 1969*

Reprint edition 1969 by Arno Press, Inc.

*

Library of Congress Catalog Card No. 73-89179

*

Reprinted from a copy in Teachers College Library

*

Manufactured in the United States of America

Editorial Note

AMERICAN EDUCATION: *Its Men, Institutions and Ideas* presents selected works of thought and scholarship that have long been out of print or otherwise unavailable. Inevitably, such works will include particular ideas and doctrines that have been outmoded or superseded by more recent research. Nevertheless, all retain their place in the literature, having influenced educational thought and practice in their own time and having provided the basis for subsequent scholarship.

Lawrence A. Cremin
Teachers College

The American College

A Criticism

THE
AMERICAN COLLEGE

A CRITICISM

BY

ABRAHAM FLEXNER

NEW YORK
THE CENTURY CO.
1908

Copyright, 1908, by
THE CENTURY CO.

———

Published October, 1908

J. F. Tapley Co
Book Manufacturers
831-833 West 31st St
New York

CONTENTS

PREFACE

This book is based on an educational experience of almost twenty years, in the course of which I prepared many pupils for college; I tried also to observe their development during and after their college careers. Subsequently I spent two years as graduate student at two different American universities, and something above a year in England and Germany, where I enjoyed opportunities for observation. I have, moreover, frequently compared notes with teachers in secondary schools, colleges, universities and professional schools, whose experience has been in some respects fuller and more

PREFACE

direct than my own.   But as their com-
munications were made in confidence,
I am compelled to forego the support
which they would lend to the argument.

ABRAHAM FLEXNER.

New York, June 20, 1908.

THE AMERICAN COLLEGE

THE
AMERICAN COLLEGE

CHAPTER I

THE PROBLEM DEFINED

I PROPOSE in this book to discuss the American college in its educational aspect. In taking this standpoint, I do not mean to imply that a college experience ought properly to contain nothing but what is explicitly or technically educational. I do mean, however, to intimate strongly that nowadays the college puts the emphasis in the wrong place; that incidental and sometimes irrelevant elements in college experience dominate the essential and fundamental educational purpose. I want to make this essential and fundamental purpose prominent in my discussion. For that reason I survey the field from the educational point of view. There is, I fancy, no danger that college life will too strictly confine itself to the same limitation; or that proper emphasis of the educational motive will altogether wither college charm. That charm is, at bottom, largely a matter of youth and the situation; it is not merely the product of triviality. Oxford life, for example, is not the less Oxford life at Balliol, where a high plane of intellectual seriousness has been long maintained.

I propose then, to analyze the educational procedure of the American college [1] from the moment when it tells the

[1] The term "college" is so loosely employed in

4

secondary school how the boy is to be
made ready for his collegiate opportunities, to the day when the Bachelor's
degree indicates that the entire process
is successfully finished. Eight years
have elapsed; during the first four the
college has directed, during the last
four completely controlled, the plastic
boy. Does the outcome bear the im-
press of a clear, consistent and valid
purpose? Does the thing prove as education to have been worth while?
These are the points at issue.

this country that it is necessary for me to indicate
the sense in which it is used in these pages. I have
in mind institutions (1) requiring for admission the
equivalent of a high school course; (2) offering the
student a considerable variety of elective courses;
(3) frequently seeking to provide opportunities
for advanced work. The indiscriminate use of the
terms college and university in America is exhaustively and lucidly discussed in the Second Annual
Report of President Henry S. Pritchett, of the
Carnegie Foundation for the Advancement of
Teaching, pp. 66–99.

Our college authorities are themselves far from happy. They dwell complacently on rapidly increasing numbers, splendid "plants" and the unchecked flow of benefactions; but there is considerable uneasiness just below the surface. The pilots are apparently not sure as to whither to steer; at times they steer for several ports at once; again, for no particular port at all. "So far as I have been able to ascertain through twenty-five years of the discussions of the Harvard board, of which I have been a member," says Mr. Charles Francis Adams,[1] "the authorities are as wide apart now as ever they were. There is no agreement; no united effort to a given end." To the same effect, President Schurman of

[1] Phi Beta Kappa address, Columbia University, June 12, 1906.

6

Cornell has recently declared:[1] "The college is without clear-cut notions of what a liberal education is and how it is to be secured, . . . and the pity of it is that this is not a local or special disability, but a paralysis affecting every college of arts in America.") The conviction that the reforms which converted the narrow academy into the "wide-open" university have not made good, is indubitably gaining ground.[2]

Profound scepticism as to the educational possibilities of the average boy is the not uncommon consequence: here are laboratories, libraries, lecture

[1] The President's Report, Cornell University, 1906–7, page 20.

[2] "Notwithstanding the fact that the American college is the most characteristic feature of the American system of education it shows to-day weaknesses which its best friends clearly recognize." Second Annual Report of President Henry S. Pritchett, Carnegie Foundation for the Advancement of Teaching, p. 80.

7

courses, calculated to meet every conceivable demand; an unheard-of accumulation of opportunities and resources; and to how little avail! Well, it must then be impossible! (The average boy is simply not educable. It is useless to repine. The capable fellow gets an education, the others get something. This is the instructor's state of mind a few years after the institution of a system recommended by the diametrically opposite course of reasoning.) For the elective system was in effect a profession of confidence in the actual capacity and probable seriousness of the average boy. It assumed that he possessed ability and might be led to develop purpose. Yet in the face of its attempt to enlist his energy in congenial effort, the college finds itself forced to a low standard. A degree may be won

8

with little or no systematic exertion. High rank is obtained with less effort than ought to be required to maintain a minimum grade.[1]   Of course there are exceptions; but the significant fact stands out, that no considerable percentage of students even try for honors, in spite of the fact that they are supposed to pursue studies for which they care and which they are going to need. Teachers in graduate and professional schools complain that college graduates of three-and-twenty are in general "thoroughly unripe"; that a college degree is far from a safe guarantee

[1] "The average amount of work done by an undergraduate in a course is less than three and a half hours a week outside the lecture room; more than half the answers from which these results are derived came from men who obtained the grade of A or B" (highest grades). Report of Harvard Committee on Improving Instruction, p. 4. There are no reasons for believing this true only at Harvard.

9

of a sufficient knowledge of the fundamental branches pursued in college with explicit reference to subsequent professional study.[1] And our college students are just as lacking in spontaneous and disinterested intellectual activity as in more strictly instrumental power and efficiency.

Comparisons are, of course, always dangerous; but I venture to declare without fear of contradiction that in

[1] These statements are partly based on the observation and judgment of a number of eminent scientists and professional men, engaged in advanced teaching, who have kindly favored me with a candid expression of their experience. They are practically unanimous in holding that the college graduate is neither a trained nor a serious worker. It is significant that almost without exception they speak of him as "settling down" in the professional school. Two of my correspondents sent me carefully compiled statistical comparisons which indicate that it is decidedly doubtful whether a college education of the type now in vogue gives a boy any *professional* advantage at all over the graduate of a good High School.

point of scholarship and trained capacity the American college graduate of three-and-twenty is sadly inferior to the German student, some three years younger. For the present, I am less concerned to explain this fact than to get it distinctly admitted. How far the college is responsible, we shall consider later; what offset ought to be entered on the other side of the ledger is just now immaterial. The important thing is to realize that the American college is deficient, and unnecessarily deficient, alike in earnestness and in pedagogical intelligence; that in consequence our college students are, and for the most part, emerge, flighty, superficial and immature, lacking, as a class, concentration, seriousness and thoroughness.[1]

[1] Every statement in this paragraph is abundantly

Does this mean that the American boy lacks intellectual capacity or that the college simply does not engage it? I hope to prove that the latter is the case; that at each of the critical junctures of the boy's education the college fails in pedagogical insight. I contend that we are not yet justified in concluding that the American boy cannot as a rule be highly trained; or that the best we can do is to coax him to polish up a bit, while, as an inducement to submit so far, he is abundantly diverted and amused. It may be, of course, that after all we shall have to accept this depressing outcome; but not at any rate until a more intelligent, systematic

sustained by the correspondence referred to in the preceding note. I may also quote further from President Pritchett's Report: "The two objections generally brought against the college to-day are vagueness of aim and lack of intellectual stamina." (p. 80.)

12

and fearless experiment has also ended in an equally negative result.

Meanwhile certain college apologists endeavor to escape the evidence of their senses by statistical demonstration of the saving virtue of a college education. Professor Cattell neatly closes this source of comfort. "The statistics," he says, "which show that college graduates are more likely than others to succeed in certain professions, are not in themselves significant. One might as well argue for compressed feet, because Chinese women who follow the practice are more likely than others to marry Mandarins. The ablest and most energetic men have gone to college, and the college has been the normal gateway to certain careers." [1]

Equally beside the mark is the argu-

[1] Science, Sept. 20, 1907.

13

ment from success in business. In some cases, the successful business man of college antecedents, merely steps into his father's shoes; in which event one is at most warranted in saying that a college education has not made the succession impossible. On the whole there is no proof that college-bred business men are more effective than the men who have worked up from the ranks. The change that frequently transforms the college graduate in his early business years suggests to me quite a different view: it is the pressure of practical life, making a man of the college dilettante. The college leaves him "soft"; he has had no such discipline, no such biting realization of consequences as one gets out in the rough and tumble of the world. The hard conditions of survival there jolt him

14

roughly, suddenly, but beneficently. Practical life with its intense, narrow urgencies binds up the shattered personality, focuses the dispersed energies. Say what one will of the world's sordidness, it is a God-send to these vagrants of the higher life.

It is, however, not impossible to admit its failure and still to acquit the college of all substantial blame. Those who take this position grant that the college is inefficient and distracted. But, they urge, it could not be otherwise: the stream can rise no higher than its source; our American life is itself distracted; mad in the pursuit of material ends. In reply, I point out that the attempt to make society the scapegoat loses sight of powerful and equally characteristic tendencies in other directions. We are by no means wholly abandoned to material ends and low standards; and the college might fairly be asked consistently to express and uphold those extant ends that are not material, those struggling standards that are not low. Now, as a matter of fact, the college does not even rise to the accepted standards of the commercial world, to whose demoralizing influence its scholarly ideals are occasionally alleged to have succumbed. For college standards of success are actually below those that prevail outside. A youth may win his degree on a showing that would in an office cost him his desk. Unquestionably certain features of American life make trouble for the schools; but is it not just as true that this same life provides education with unparalleled opportunities? An education condemned to a formal and

16

sterile routine might hesitate under existing circumstances to compete with outside attractions. But formality and routine attach to education to-day only so far as education chooses to retain them. They are needless; they are alien. Our life fairly tingles with the romance of activity. Science, industry, libraries, cheap books, cheap transportation, close contact with social and international problems—all make grist for the school mill. To no previous age has such a variety of interests been so accessible. The society which has put such material, such stimuli at the service of the school-master, has given him far more than it has taken away.

Finally, there are critics who see in the situation only the breakdown of the effort to modernize the college curriculum. Their remedy is a retreat: "the resuscitation of the all-around man through the compulsory study of Latin or Greek to the day of graduation." [1] Such a proposal ignores altogether the reality and validity of the factors that destroyed the old-fashioned college. The classical curriculum went to pieces, because it had long since served its purpose. It cannot be put together again; the suggestion is utterly futile. An arbitrary discipline of the classical type is enforceable only where it has an adequate sanction in social regard, and a real point of discharge in the social organization. Men must believe in it; something must depend on it. This is still to a considerable extent the case in Germany. There they believe that a training in the classical languages actually matters, that the classical disci-

[1] Adams, Phi Beta Kappa address.

pline does for youth some indispensable thing that nothing else can do equally well. The schools, the learned professions, the government, the family still hold more or less together on this point. Under such circumstances, a prolonged and for some purposes effective training can be got out of the classics. The situation is indeed changing in Germany,—rapidly changing, as things go there; but for the present, the traditional education is the main and in some directions the only door to preferment. It is very different with us; the conditions under which the classics can be made the basis of a prolonged discipline simply do not exist here. We do not believe in their disciplinary efficacy or necessity; nor are we likely to be persuaded of it. Nothing tangible depends on Greek and Latin; they lead nowhere. There is no conviction—social, professional, official, strong enough to sustain their use as the backbone of the educational system: hence, the futility of our classical instruction.

But there is another and even deeper objection to the proposed revival of Greek and Latin in this rôle. Sheer discipline, whether of the classical or any other kind, cannot give us the type of educated man that modern society wants. I say it leads nowhere; it does not connect individuals with concrete opportunities. I do not mean this formula to exhaust the province of college education; but so much at least a college education must do. The classical discipline can take no account of this central fact. It goes its way regardless of particular situations. It tends therefore to the over-production of educated men whose training leaves them high in the air without a parachute to get to earth in.[1]

My argument, therefore, contemplates not the abandonment, but the completer working-out of modern educational tendencies. The new insight is indeed fragmentary and unorganized; but it is on the right track. It aims to vitalize education; to bring the boy's powers to bear; to connect the individual with life. Our part is not to antagonize a movement so clearly sound and inevitable, but having grasped its purport, to assist its complete realization.

[1] It is perhaps needless to point out that I do not mean to discriminate against the classics as permanent and fruitful objects of mature study. Elsewhere I have said that, in this respect, they "take their chances with the rest." Here I simply deny that the classical grind accomplishes what it is theoretically expected to do. Fortunately the fate and currency of classic thought are in no wise dependent on the compulsory learning of the rudiments of Latin and Greek Grammar by successive generations of reluctant boys.

CHAPTER II

THE American college is not, like the common school, indigenous to American soil. It did not spring up to meet a native need. It was imported to meet a need that the colonists brought with them. Hence, a conservative, not an adaptive institution, it bound the emigrant to his past. This it was designed to do. The settlement of the New World was not, indeed, undertaken in an experimental spirit. With rare exceptions the colonists were not pioneers in a speculative sense. They were troubled with no doubts as to what was true and right. They

22

merely sought a place to maintain, believe and practice an already fully articulate creed. It was soon observed that transplantation into a strange environment threatened Puritanism with dangers, insidious and unforeseen. The absence of persecution operated to loosen the inner bond; moreover, pioneer life was not without novel temptations from the outside. The college was set up in order to resist these tendencies; to secure the type; to renew and fortify the old English Puritan;[1] and it played no insignificant part in establishing the breed, despite native

[1] "After God had carried us safe to New England and we had builded our houses, provided necessaries for our livelihood, reared convenient places for God's worship, and setled the civill Government, one of the next things we longed for and looked after was to advance learning and perpetuate it to posterity, dreading to leave an illiterate ministry to the churches, when our present ministers shall lie in the dust." New England's First Fruits.

23

forces working in the opposite direction.

Its conservative office the college continued to discharge amidst fairly congenial conditions, almost to our own times. The gradual expansion of the curriculum, in the meanwhile, betokened no radical enlargement of horizon. Increasing complexity of life, progressive amelioration of manners, made lawyers and gentlemen almost as necessary as clergymen. The college supplied them. They were cast in pretty much the same old die; at any rate, imbued with pretty much the same old spirit. The necessary extension of discipline was effected, without fundamentally altering its point of view. In course of time the college became somewhat more human, somewhat more gracious, somewhat broader in scope and interest,

24

but hardly less conservative. It still looked mainly to the past.

In the last half century, however, this situation has markedly changed. Two factors, science and democracy, have completely transformed our atmosphere and ideals. So congenially have these two forces been engaged throughout the western world in the task of reconstruction, that the connection between them seems too deep for accident. Their conquests have, of course, not been altogether easy. Habits, vested interests, institutions — among them, the college itself—stubbornly resisted change. Direct action upon social and political machinery and ideas thus soon developed definite limitations. Reform, after all, amounts merely to poking the fire from the top. Attention was then, somewhat tardily,

directed to education, which had hith-
erto followed conventional lines. The
fire must be poked from below. Education gets in this way a creative and
adaptive function, in reference to a new
social and intellectual ideal. It ceases
to be the bulwark of creeds,—philosophical, scientific, theological,—whose doom
has been pronounced. The schools no
longer furnish asylum to ideas that cannot maintain themselves in the open.
They become, instead, engines for the
completer subversion of the passing order, for the more thorough diffusion of
light and air. This transformation of
the schools has not been everywhere
equally rapid and complete. It has
been bitterly antagonized at some
points in Germany; in England, the
fate of the Public Schools and the ancient Universities is still involved in

grave doubt; it is still a question how far they will lend themselves to current needs. The American college was summarily required to make a decisive choice; to readjust itself or to go by the board. A variety of needs, many of them in conflict with its traditions, and all going far beyond them, had to be cared for. For a time the college resisted, at least retarded, the movement; in the end, to save itself, it executed a right-about. American college history has been made rapidly since 1870. The general causes, common, as has been pointed out, to the entire western world, have been in this country accelerated by local influences. Here a vast population but recently freed from disability of one sort or another found itself in a highly favorable environment just at the moment when science was suggesting to industry quick and effective methods of turning the situation to account. In its turn industry has repaid the laboratory by testing its conclusions and propounding new and stimulating problems. But educational interest has by no means confined itself to the physical sciences. The same eager spirit has penetrated other realms; it is re-writing history, re-conceiving social theory, working-out a nearer and more cogent standpoint in philosophy. All this many-sided activity comes to a focus in the college. The curriculum struggles to embrace every topic of serious intellectual or practical concern; it calls for all possible varieties of individual capacity and preference. The reconstructive function of the college is still further emphasized by the development, in close connection with the college, of graduate schools, borrowing the technique of research perfected in Germany, and largely devoted to the discovery and circulation of new truth. The contents of college instruction are thus, like the waters of a mountain lake, always in process of fresh replacement. The college can never again be restricted to conservation of a hard-and-fast type, individual and social. It has become one of the main agents of progress and change.

Structurally the college that now accommodates interests so various consists of a large number of highly specialized and separate departments, each striving to be more or less completely representative of its own field: a department of physics, a department of classics, a department of history, a department of mathematics, etc. They no longer all revolve around a central sun; they do not even freely intersect. Rather, the several departments lie side by side, of equal dignity with each other. The entire structure is capped by professional and technical schools of law, medicine, engineering, agriculture, etc. One or another of these features may be absent or rudimentary; but all together they form the structural ideal towards which the American college unmistakably strives.

The changed significance of the B.A. degree tells this story in detail. Forty years ago the Bachelor's degree conveyed a specific and practically invariable meaning. There was one narrow path to academic confirmation; every candidate had to traverse it. Perhaps the college graduate did not expect to be a lawyer or a clergyman; he had, however, to be content with an education strictly relevant only to these two learned callings. A cultivated man was one who, whatever his ignorance or limitations in other directions, had enjoyed a liberal education of this description. The classics were the back-bone of the college curriculum; they were supplemented by the cut and dried philosophy and rhetoric then current, some mathematics and bookish science, and an occasional dip into modern literature. To a limited extent, the individual was even then permitted in a few colleges to modify this scheme; but, in general, the bulk of the instruction was the same for all. Its spirit was unmistakably rigorous and partial. As against this uniform and unambiguous procedure, it would nowadays tax the ingenuity of a professional mathematician to calculate the number of study-combinations that qualify for the B.A. degree. The Bachelor's degree now indicates simply three or four years of study in some line or lines appropriate to some intellectual concern or other. On the face of the diploma there is usually nothing to show where in the wide universe of science or scholarship the individual's preference lay.[1] He may have adhered closely to the traditional classical scheme; or he may have entirely ignored the humanities in favor of physical science; or he may have ignored all the sciences but one; or he may have cultivated philosophy or modern literature; or finally he may have made a sort of gentlemanly "grand tour"

[1] A few colleges confer different degrees (B. Sc., B. Lit. etc.); but each of these is still quite vague.

through the capitals of the chief provinces of intellectual interest.

An analogous transformation has somewhat more tardily and less radically taken place in Germany. I have pointed out that essentially the same influences are at work there as here: social democracy and scientific industrialism. Between them they have largely reconstructed an institution far more refractory than the American college. For the classical gymnasium long enjoyed a legal monopoly: it was the only door to a professional career. A bitter struggle with many ups and downs has at length deprived it of its exclusive privileges. Three paths have been cut, where there was formerly only one: the Realgymnasium with Latin and no Greek, and Realschule with neither

Latin nor Greek, stand nominally in respect to subsequent opportunities on almost the same footing as the historic classical gymnasium.[1] The German scheme is of course more guarded and less flexible than our elective system; but it proves the acceptance of a similar view of the business of higher education in modern society. "The schools," says Paulsen,[2] "cannot tear themselves loose from the general march of culture. Classical study formed originally the entire content of all higher training; in the nineteenth century, however, it necessarily declined into simply an essential element in this training. The time is coming—and the most recent

[1] I say "nominally" because a powerful caste feeling still operates in favor of the classical gymnasium. Similarly in the English Public Schools the "classical side" enjoys distinct and effective social prestige as against the "modern side."

[2] Das Deutsche Bildungswesen, p. 139.

ordinances indicate this point of view —when it will not even be regarded as a necessary ingredient of a liberal education."

Pedagogically, this development means that higher education which formerly derived its goal and chief material from humanistic culture is now coextensive with the reach and interest of intelligence. Mentally and socially, culture in the narrow sense was an aristocratic conception: mentally, because of its marked predilection for literary and artistic forms of activity and expression; socially, because it detached a learned class. The old-fashioned college of limited scope and fixed curriculum thus made sharp distinctions of dignity and value within the intellectual field; its emphasis was aesthetic.

Now, by way of contrast the modern

college is impartial, catholic, democratic. Its concern is the whole field; its responsibility and duty to society at large, not to a certain section thereof. It embraces therefore all types of intellectual capacity, all the characteristic processes and activities of social expression and growth: science, industry, trade, laws, institutions are its objects not less worthily than art, literature, philosophy. It makes no question of precedence among them; amid conditions where all are badly needed, it holds it idle to indulge arbitrary preferences; wasteful and disturbing to interfere needlessly with the natural outlet of the youth's energy, by a sort of academic "protective tariff" that tempts or drives him into an uncongenial expression. The list of things socially, hence educationally, worth while thus extends indefinitely: truth, beauty, yes; but equally, comfort, health, wholesome food, well-governed towns with pure water and clean streets. Higher education covers the entire social field, and not merely a detached portion. Its problem is the effective exploitation of the individual on the basis of this varied social opportunity and need. The educational premium on particular forms of endowment has disappeared; the inducement to particular forms of expression has been withdrawn. More and more the college takes its cue from the individual himself. It means to discern significant tendencies in him, to convert these into actual power. Education is no longer a formal discipline, but rather a concrete device to facilitate the assertion of individual capacity in terms of rational activities. This is the serious significance of the extended scope of the American college and of the elective system; this, the meaning of libraries, laboratories and museums constantly multiplying and enlarging. The college has come down from the mountain; it dwells among men.

The outcome of a successful education on these lines is not approximation of the individual to a pre-conceived type of culture, but primarily his appropriate and effective orientation in society. The conception is thoroughly democratic. The student's destination is motived from within; there are no arbitrary obstacles to congenial self-realization; there is no vocational stigma. The sole criteria are social need in the first place, adequate scope for the individual in the second. The thing is to secure the frictionless rise of the individual to his level. There he means most to society, and life means most to him. The modern college undertakes to create the conditions in which this result may take place. So far as its resources permit, it slights nothing: it provides preliminary training indiscriminately for lawyer, doctor, clergyman, technician, scholar, merchant. Whatever the verdict passed on the efficacy of the educational application, nowhere else have American energy and intelligence achieved a more solid result than in this widening of the scope of higher education, in this frank recognition of the culture value and dignity of science and the useful arts.

The transformation which I have now described has occurred in all characteristically American institutions to the extent that their resources have permitted them to take part in the movement. Lack of means rather than difference of pedagogical aspiration or principle distinguishes as a rule the colleges that remain closer to the point of origin. Even as it is, uniformity in certain respects already practically prevails. The entrance requirements are about identical; the elective system is well nigh universal; and colleges too poor to maintain a regular graduate department still like to entertain a few graduate students. The general drift is therefore towards the type exemplified by the radical and comprehensive institutions. Among them it seems to me impossible to discover any far-reaching pedagogical variations. They exhibit no considerable or significant peculiarities of range or structure.

Differences of age between them count for comparatively little. The older foundations all necessarily developed along similar lines; while the most recent, though enjoying a free hand, have been in the main content to reproduce what they found at the moment in possession of the field. These latter institutions started up complete; hence they could entertain no deep-seated doubts; try no extensive or novel educational experiments. They assumed that, on the whole, "whatever is, is best," sacrificing, as it seems to me, the tremendous opportunities that in a scientific age belong to the country and the institution that have no history. In consequence, they have increased the quantity rather than changed the quality of the college output. To the same category belong certain institutions, long retarded

by poverty, which have employed the
increased resources suddenly received
in recent years in uncritically repro-
ducing the college type developed in
the Eastern states. Fortunately local
conditions have to a certain extent di-
versified their activities; but their institutional ambition has been much too
largely absorbed in the endeavor to rival
or duplicate that which it would have
been far more wholesome to reconsider.[1]
Even in a fresh field, like the college
education of women, where the absence
of a traditional or conventional structure created an ideal opportunity for
experiment, we have escaped the em-

[1] Decidedly the most promising novelty is Princeton's preceptorial system, which I notice more fully
later (p. 207). The University of Chicago offers
certain original features (e.g. its four continuous
terms, the distinction between Junior and University
Colleges), but it can hardly be said that as yet any
definite results have been realized from them.

barrassments of freedom by devolving upon girls the education that has proved of doubtful fitness for boys. An astonishing degree of sameness, an astonishing lack of experimental originality, mark the entire situation. College pride affects indeed to discriminate nicely between the Yale and Harvard man, the Vassar and Wellesley girl. We need not take this sort of thing seriously. These subtle distinctions may be safely ignored. The only significant marks to be observed are traceable to individual teachers. Here and there a strong man breaks through and makes a permanent impression on the students who come under him. But this phenomenon is quite consistent with general institutional uniformity. The rough but effective tests of life discover no essential differences in training, type or capacity in the college product.

I do not mean of course to overlook altogether such differences as actually exist. It is worth while to examine here how far they extend. Harvard, Cornell, Michigan are, for instance, pronounced and unequivocal, Yale and Princeton more conservative, in attitude. The latter have moved less rapidly, though in the same path. No college has permanently resisted the characteristic modern tendencies; no college has revolted; no college has proposed a radically distinct conception or solution of educational problems. The differences reside not in the things done, but in the length to which they are carried. Harvard and Michigan have evidently enjoyed being thoroughly modern; they manifest no regrets. Yale and Prince-

44

ton have followed in the same procession at a somewhat irregular pace. They have not wanted to stay behind; they have failed to discover a more satisfactory alternative route; they have only gone more slowly,—at heart, unconvinced, I suspect, and as I shall try to show, in some respects justifiably unconvinced. When, for instance, Harvard introduced the elective system, its action showed the courage and the joy of conviction: it really introduced it. Yale compromised. The Yale system is halting, piecemeal, a grudging attempt to make an old-fashioned curriculum melt imperceptibly into the elective scheme. But the difference between the two is not a difference of principle. When the Yale system gets into full swing, it is practically just as unorganized, just as innocent of controlling educational purpose as the Harvard system, even though it lacks the Harvard abandon at the start; it is not, in a word, redeemed by its tardiness or its few external checks.

So again, as regards the relation of college and secondary school, Harvard's attitude is clean-cut; a sharp horizontal line divides the two. The moment the boy crosses the dividing line, he enters a different world; the line is drawn straight across. At Yale and Princeton they draw the line obliquely; the required studies of the high-school project into the college, and there break off one by one. But the difference is not educationally profound; it matters little how the line is drawn, whether horizontally or obliquely. All these institutions are equally in error in their conception of secondary education; alike they draw a line, where nature intends a web.

It will have been observed that I speak of the college and of that alone. I intend thus to discriminate the college as such from the additions and developments that have converted it into a university. My business is with the college, as a place for the final training of boys, not with the entire system of special or advanced schools that cluster about or spring from it. I do not now question the wisdom of the policy that from mere colleges developed our present universities. But I wish to emphasize strongly the view that this development has neither destroyed the responsibilities of the college nor shifted them to some other quarter. These responsibilities have indeed become greater, just by reason of the heavier super-

47

structure that now rests upon the college foundation. The heart of the university is the college. No separate department can work well if that heart works ill. The ultimate integrity of university performance depends on the way the college attends to its proper business; that business constitutes in almost every instance, historically and practically, a first lien on the resources of the institution.[1]

With the technical, graduate and professional departments which belong to the American university we have therefore no concern, except in so far as

[1] The exceptions are institutions like the Johns Hopkins, Leland Stanford Jr., the University of Chicago, Bryn Mawr, the resources of which have never belonged to the college alone; as their graduate departments were established at the very beginning, they stand in this matter on the same footing as the college.

they react upon the college. They grow out of the college; they lean on it. But at no point is anyone of them identical with it. The work of the college is done, when their work begins. For them the college has a specific task to do; they set up—each of them—certain objective requirements that college training must satisfy. Of course, it must do something more, too. Its duty is not confined to the preliminary grounding of prospective lawyers, doctors, and archæologists, each in the elements fundamental to his own career. But the point I now make is, that even in reference to the career in which a subsequent discipline is continuous with college work, though the two somewhere merge, they do not coincide. The isolation in which I propose to dis-

cuss the college is no mere abstraction:
it is fair to the actual facts; it is essential to clear thought.

A brief consideration of the chief
products of the advanced schools
will make this point evident. Out
of material, supposedly shaped up
by the college, the law school makes
lawyers. The end is definite, practical; the means, direct and concrete.
That method is preferred which
attains the desired result most effectively. There lies the virtue of the
case system—a system which cuts loose
from formal text-books and distills the
juice of typical cases. From the first
the student is in contact with actual issues, with court process, with trial machinery: every principle is concretely
embodied in illustrative fact. The case
system trains lawyers,—not jurists.

Jurisprudence in a comparative or philosophical sense cuts no figure. A highly trained and resourceful legal intelligence immediately available in the courts or the office issues from the law school. The clinic, the laboratory, an adaptation of the case method, achieve a similar result in medicine. It does not follow that our best professional schools despise the scientific or philosophic spirit or expect the individual to go ahead without it. The truth is that, for the time being, they assume the free scientific and philosophic discipline as done. They take for granted a certain division of labor. The responsibility for a training that underlies every form of specialization, that relates the individual career with the civilization in which it is enveloped, belongs—so the professional school assumes—to the college. There is no question of any considerable overlapping here.

Similar considerations eliminate the graduate school too from the present discussion. Superficially, its relation to the college seems more intimate. It does not start abruptly, like the law school, for instance. It continues college pursuits,—with a difference: breaking them up, refining upon them. There are few graduate occupations that do not thus run straight back to undergraduate roots. Nevertheless, despite continuity of subject matter there is a decisive change of attitude. The two departments are really commissioned to do two entirely different things. Take their respective attitudes in reference to a particular interest,— say, history. The undergraduate enters college with a meagre outline acquaintance with ancient history or the history of England and the United States, not necessarily—and hence rarely—both. The tasks of the next few years are quickly set: the teacher's, to stimulate interest, develop connections and relations; the student's, to increase his knowledge of the facts, to cultivate an inclination to construe social problems largely and sympathetically. Incidentally, something may be done to initiate the beginner into methods and technique; but—and this is nowadays so apt to be forgotten!—never at the expense of the main business of college history teaching. Now, the graduate student has presumably left this stage behind him. He is supposed to know; to be able to survey the field at large. Hence he betakes himself off to some unoccupied corner: there he delves for ore or fossils. His interest is mainly critical and productive. Technique,— at best an interesting incident to the undergraduate, introduced by way of stimulating interest or promoting intelligent judgment of evidence—is everything to the graduate investigator. Whether he is to search forever or some day to become a mere teacher, according to current conception of what becomes a graduate student, his main business for three years is microscopic,—and in conclusion a thesis, making as much as possible of it. I do not undertake to say whether this dispensation is wise or unwise: the point is that it is at least distinct from the sort of thing that is cut out for the undergraduate.

From the educational standpoint, then, the graduate school is on the plane of the professional schools. Its concern is equally definite, special, practical. The graduate school trains specialists, as the law school trains specialists. It makes no essential difference that its specialists are scientists or scholars, instead of lawyers. Mere remoteness from so-called practical life is beside the point. After all, that is something one can never be certain about: the most abstruse and disinterested researches may astonish us by cutting straight across the common routine of daily life! Some chemical dreamer will one day drop a grain of starch into the housekeeper's lap! However this may be, the discipline of the scholar is as narrowly conceived as that of the lawyer *in reference to its end.* That is the decisive point. The relation of vocation or interest to training is the same; the presupposition in reference to previous education is identical.

The point at which the professional schools part from the college can then be distinctly marked on the map: it is the point at which the student as such becomes of less importance than the pursuit as such. Of course neither element need ever entirely disappear. The objective aim furnishes content, stimulus, standard to the boy; the human element has an adapting rôle to play, when science is severest. But the difference in emphasis is nevertheless so pronounced that the entire complexion of education changes between the college and the later schools. Throughout the college the student is prospective man, not simply prospective professional man; in the graduate schools the student as individual practically ceases to count: there the standards, demands, ideals, are pitilessly objective.

Between the attitude and resources which I have now described and the college product as characterized in the preceding chapter, a startling incongruity appears. It strikes one with fresh force whenever one turns from the college outfit or catalogue to the concrete manifestations of college life. The two somehow do not fit. On the one side, a formidable array of scholars and scientists, libraries, laboratories, publications; on the other, a large, miscellaneous student body, marked by an immense sociability on a common-place basis and widespread absorption in trivial and boyish interests. How are we to account for the disparity? Clearly the college fails to enlist a respectable portion of the youth's total energy in intellectual effort; either its sincerity or its pedagogical intelligence is discredited by the occupations and diversions which it finds not incompatible with its standards and expectations. It is easy to say that these by-products are the causes of pedagogical inefficiency; but it is obvious on reflection that they must be equally its results. Once started, indeed, they develop rapidly on their own account, steadily encroaching; but they could not have started, had the college had definite aims, enforced through an adequate educational procedure. Hence, badly as administrative vigor is required, it is alone far from meeting the fundamental need. It is comparatively simple to extirpate those who appear to be the weaker brethren; but it is not a whit more intelligent than to pull every aching tooth.

I shall endeavor in the following chapters to analyze the express pedagogical policy of the college at each of the critical junctures of the boy's education in the hope of reaching the ultimate causes of the discrepancy between what the college undertakes and what it achieves.

CHAPTER III

THE COLLEGE AND THE SECONDARY SCHOOL

A STUDY of the educational efficiency of the college necessarily includes the preparatory school in which the college is really the controlling stockholder. The connection is inevitable; a supply of fit material is thereby ensured. Whatever the contract which the college undertakes, its fulfillment within the appointed time depends, in the first place, on the ability of the preparatory school to deliver the necessary raw material in the right shape. Now, that there may be no question, the college practically de-

prives the sub-contractor of discretion.[1]
Its specifications—the so-called entrance requirements—are full and precise; it reserves the right by means of

[1] It is true that the College Entrance Board is
made up of representatives of both colleges and
secondary schools; but this Board is an examining
board only: it has absolutely nothing to do with
determining the entrance requirements of the several
colleges. It simply conducts examinations in the various subjects forming the college entrance lists. The
entrance requirements were arranged by the colleges
themselves long before the Board was thought of
and in all essential respects remain now what they
were then. Various conferences have, indeed, from
time to time suggested modifications of detail that
have been generally adopted; but nothing of fundamental importance has thus been achieved. Besides,
the colleges still largely maintain their own separate
examinations, in which the secondary schools have
no part whatsoever; the colleges accept the College
Entrance Board examinations as equivalent to their
own. Further: in making up the Board questions,
the college influence strongly predominates; each set
of questions is prepared by a committee, to which
the colleges contribute two representatives, the secondary schools one. Unquestionably the Board has
been the means of eliminating a good deal of capri-
cious and needless variation. On the whole, however,
their examinations are not free from the objections
urged in this chapter to a system of examination by

entrance examinations to reject every
proffered candidate failing to conform
to them. There is no question as to
this domination in case of the academy
expressly devoted to college preparation; how stands it with the high
schools? Now, I do not deny that the
independent high schools, at present our
most vigorous and valuable agencies of
secondary education—originally influenced the colleges powerfully. They
first created the "modern side"; in a
measure, their popularity forced the

an external and necessarily mechanical agency. As
long as the College Entrance Board remains such an
agency, it cannot fundamentally affect matters. This
is practically admitted by the Secretary in his Sev-
enth Annual Report (1907, p. 44): "as the number
of candidates examined by the Board increases, the
quality of the average candidate's preparation is
steadily deteriorating." The Board has, on the other
hand, possibilities in other directions; and once in-
fected with a more experimental and genuine pedagogical spirit, might become the means of radical,
even if gradual, reform.

colleges to accept modern subjects on a par with the classics and mathematics. So far the colleges surrendered to the high school; but subsequent moves have reversed the situation. The definite collegiate formulations of what is wanted in each subject have reacted on these schools, practically determining for them the spirit, method and contents of their instruction. A specious line of argument is thus costing the high schools the freedom they used so well; there is only one right way, say the colleges, of teaching a subject, whether the boy is going to college or not. The high schools assent; in the next moment, the college defines that one way; and its control threatens to become just as complete and pedantic in the domain of science and modern languages, as it has always been in the classical realm. A strong and wholly regrettable tendency has thus developed in the direction of accepting the college entrance requirements as conclusively marking off the proper sphere of secondary instruction and as authoritatively prescribing how this work ought to be carried on.

The two institutions are thus essentially subject to one authority, or, more correctly, the secondary school, at least so far as it aims to prepare boys for college, is now largely controlled by the college and in its interest; despite which, as we shall see, they do not organically fuse. Beyond the secondary school, the college has not yet sought to pierce. The elementary school has not yet been brought within the college "sphere of influence." The college makes no demand on the secondary school which compels the secondary school in its turn to influence elementary education. In consequence, the elementary school has enjoyed some freedom for experimentation. There is a place in it for zeal, originality, enthusiasm; there alone a purely educational interest finds scope. In the high school there is less and less room for pedagogical initiative; there never has been much in the college. Hence elementary education, though chargeable with certain crudities and absurdities, has shown the capacity to profit by its own mistakes; it has undeniably advanced, and that, without pressure from above.

This is the initial pedagogical blunder of the college; it unwittingly snubs elementary education. It so defines and applies its admission requirements

5   65

that their fulfillment becomes wholly a matter for the secondary school without reliance upon, or organic connection with, the elementary school. Utter waste of the earlier school years does not militate against entering college; a wise use of them does not help the candidate, whose fate is wholly dependent on literal compliance with terms that can be best met by cramming a few years just before entering college. As a matter of fact, the early years are of the most vital consequence to an education that proposes the exploitation of the individual on native lines. Such an education must begin early; the ultimate fullness and definiteness of individual life are conditioned on seizing and utilizing the instincts as they go by. The tiny rills must be protected near their source, their channels cleared, if they are ever to form a clear stream, instead of losing themselves in a vague, oozy marsh. Now, of the child the college takes no notice—direct or indirect—during the fruitful and fateful years, when the instincts open, tarry for a moment, then close unsatisfied and disappear. Thus the first break in education takes place; childhood is detached; to be neglected, if it so happens; in any event, not to connect organically with the really dignified stage that opens when the serious business of college preparation begins.

But whatever its omissions in respect to elementary education, the college appears by its assumption of control to appreciate its essential continuity with the secondary school. In the matter of this control a distinction may be made between the more conservative

67

colleges — (Yale, Princeton) — which practically insist upon a fixed and uniform course of preparatory study and the more radical institutions, (Harvard, Columbia, Michigan, Cornell) which permit a limited amount of choice. The distinction does not go beyond a narrowly limited choice of studies; in the teaching of the subjects chosen none of the colleges allow the least latitude. That, as we shall see, is everywhere determined by the minute prescriptions of the college catalogue, backed up by the entrance examinations. We are not, therefore, to understand that in one case the preparatory school is fettered, in the other, free; the difference is only that the conservative colleges fetter the preparatory school from start to finish; the radical colleges put on the same fetters, after allowing a choice between certain alternatives.

The unfitness of the rigid and uniform preparatory course, prescribed by the conservative institutions, may be readily demonstrated. Indeed the very arguments and considerations that have led them to loosen up their own curricula apply with equal or greater force to the secondary period. I have said that the college controls the secondary school in order to make sure that it will get what it needs. What then does it need? In the first place, the boy must be in secure possession of a certain amount of knowledge. We shall assume that the required preparatory course assures this. Now, under the old regime, in which a fixed college course followed a fixed preparatory course, this was perhaps enough: the

boy who had learned in the secondary
school the elements of Latin, mathematics, etc., could enter college classes
in the same subjects and proceed without break or jar. But now that the
elective system is practically universal,
the possession of a certain amount of
knowledge is insufficient. Neither
knowledge of the prescribed rudiments,
nor the discipline supposedly attained in
the course of acquiring this elementary
acquaintance, equips the youth to meet
the novel responsibility laid upon him
by the elective system. He has hereto-
fore studied one set of subjects; suddenly the elective system requires him
to select and organize for himself an
appropriate and probably very different set. He has had to study for four
years Latin, Greek, mathematics: how
does this enable him to find his way

intelligently in totally distinct realms of activity and interest? How does it help even to locate the realm in which he is to be at home? Under the elective system, whether in the outright form, in use at Harvard and Michigan, or in the restricted form in vogue at Yale and Princeton, the main value of preparatory education must turn upon the help it affords the student in the emergency, upon which the outcome of his college education depends: the one question is now—has he been so trained that he can and will make a series of intelligent and rationally connected choices?

The hard and fast preparatory school combination leaves this problem untouched. It affords the student no chance to disclose the capacity or to develop the purpose upon which shortly the college is going to presume; it requires the secondary school teacher to be a drill master, without responsibility for the liberation or definition of the pupil's significant tendencies. Under the most favorable conditions these tendencies are ignored; under less favorable conditions they are actually suppressed. The plan we are considering thus fails to effect an organic connection between preparatory education and college opportunity: it is thoroughly illogical and unscientific.

The other type,—more radical, endeavors to avoid this rupture by extending the region of choice backward into the preparatory school. It is very rightly held that if the college student is to undertake the conduct of his own subsequent education, he must have previously developed a guiding consciousness of his own line. He must be headed the right way; he must be able to take his bearings; he must be trained actively to handle himself in a concrete situation rather than just passively to "learn." This is the indispensable preliminary to the efficient operation of any sort of elective system, the very least that the college can require of the secondary school.

Now, in order to enable the secondary school to locate the individual and to carry forward his development on appropriate lines, the radical colleges have made away with the traditional curriculum imposed indiscriminately on all alike. They have substituted for it a considerable range of choices from among which a curriculum adapted to their purpose, can, it is supposed, be framed. Does this scheme, plainly devised as a basis for the elective system, accomplish what it intends? I shall try to show that its flexibility is apparent rather than real; it is therefore at this point the less necessary to point out that even flexibility will not alone solve the problem that the college elective system imposes on the secondary school.

For the purposes of clearness and concreteness, I shall discuss from this point of view the Harvard entrance requirements; what is true of them applies with practically equal force to the requirements of Cornell, Columbia, Michigan, and others.

Thirty-odd subjects covering an exceedingly wide field enter into the Harvard entrance scheme; many of them are there for the first time accorded academic recognition. Side by side

74

with time-honored veterans like the classics and mathematics, newcomers like music and blacksmithing are made at home. To each subject is assigned a specific value, estimated in points, according to its difficulty or importance: English counts 4, Elementary Latin 4, Algebra 2, Music 2, Chemistry 2, etc. For admission, a total of 26 points must be secured. Here, then, one might say, is abundant elasticity; even should the boy enter the preparatory school unexplored or untrained, aimlessness must there cease: for Harvard imposes a definite task on secondary education and provides an organizable curriculum whereby to attain it.

Alas, it does no such thing! Closer inspection discloses the fact that what one hand offers, the other withdraws. The elective range, within which the school is supposed to accomplish the student's continuous and purposeful development, is largely nominal. Of the 26 points needed for entrance, at least 18 are absorbed by studies required of everybody alike; that is to say, about 70 per cent. of the work is rigidly pre-ordained for all comers. Prescribed are English, Latin or Greek, French or German, Ancient or Modern History, Algebra, Geometry and one Science. Now, consider this conglomeration from the standpoint of college need; is it possible to see in it any pervading purpose? To what has it reference? Certainly not to the ascertaining or definition of individual power, which the college pre-supposes. Nor does it, as a collection, embody the elements underlying the general social life, and therefore, claiming the warrant of social necessity. The fact is, no rational basis whatsoever can be made out for it, either from the individualistic or social standpoint. It is, in the main, simply the old fixed curriculum that is deemed to have been displaced; an arbitrary, though easily explicable, combination of unrelated and jarring items: English, for example, enters for practical reasons; Latin or Greek is a concession to the educational Tories; science, an offset, to placate the radicals; and mathematics offers homage to "drill." Every item is a separate scrap; the whole is a patchwork, suggesting in its method of composition, a political platform rather than a rational educational program.

Nothing better illustrates the illogicality of this curriculum than the disposition it makes of Latin; and what is true of Latin holds also for Greek. In the college its study is optional; a clear intimation that the college does not regard a knowledge of Latin as of vital importance in modern life. On what ground is it required in the secondary school? The stipulated amount is not severe enough to constitute a discipline; its outcome in knowledge is both insignificant and misleading. Educationally two courses are open; one, that proposed by Mr. Adams, the restoration of required Latin or Greek to the college, thus securing for it the time and continuity necessary in order to realize its value as discipline—a step involving, of course, a complete abandonment of the present college attitude; the other, the excision of the present futile fragment from the preparatory school, where it obstructs a reorganization of the curriculum on vital lines, and accustoms the pupil to low standards and evasion. If the classics are to furnish a valuable or essential discipline, their pursuit must be genuine and prolonged; if, on the other hand, the secondary school is to undertake to organize the boy around important personal and social activities, the classics must take their chances with other subjects. Of the two alternatives here presented, the latter, in my judgment, embodies the correct principle, and at any rate is alone consistent with the modern idea. From the time when Latin ceased to be compulsory in the college, its days in secondary education were numbered. That it still survives must be ascribed partly to vagueness of conception, partly to lack of courage, both of which have co-operated in making up this required list.

It is true that 30 per cent. of the student's energies is not yet bespoken. If not impossible, it is very improbable that the choices left will be employed to contrive a coherent curriculum. The purposelessness of the required group encourages dispersion. The boy still needs seven or eight "points." He does not have to choose them in harmony with that portion of the required subjects that represents his real purpose; for so far he has been under no constraint to uncover or develop a purpose. Instead, therefore, of now at last concentrating the residue of his energies at a significant point, nothing prevents him from using his remaining choices to spread himself still farther and this is precisely what happens: "acquaintance with a hundred things and

mastery of none," "flabby inefficiency,"
"loose vagueness and inaccuracy"—in
such terms Prof. Münsterberg frankly
describes the incoming Freshman,[1]
whose training has been dictated by
and has conformed to the entrance requirements. The reason is plain.
The boy has already been shattered;
dispersed among a variety of arbitrary
tasks, that cannot be made to play upon
each other, to bend to him, or to connect
with actual experience. It is impossible at the last moment to introduce a
principle of unity into an inherently
structureless scheme. The prescribed
studies determine the entire situation:
time, energy, interest are lacking to
redeem it. For the most part, therefore, no fight is made; the exigencies of
the school curriculum, the boy's con-

[1] Science, Sept. 20, 1907.

venience, decide the "free" choices. Incidentally we may remark, in leaving this aspect of the subject, the college here pays a penalty for its neglect of elementary education: what is valuable in its prescribed requirements belongs of right largely to the earlier stages and could be there much more effectively achieved. Thus the open space in the secondary school might be considerably enlarged. But such a transfer cannot be effected so long as the college holds the latter to its instructions through a system of examinations that necessarily impoverish elementary and congest secondary instruction.

One can guess the answer of the college to this criticism: the required studies constitute the backbone which holds the thing together. Wipe them out, follow the optional system to its logical conclusion, and you have as many curricula as you have boys. A school becomes a collection of atoms, flying apart, like a freely expanding gas.

That a common substratum must be laid, I agree; that the entrance requirements furnish the needed substratum, I just as unhesitatingly deny. An education that proposes to mediate between realizable individuals and the environment conditioning their realization has in the first instance to ask what are then the indispensable stipulations that the environment makes: these must constitute the vertebral column of the educational system. Can the ingredients of the required list fairly lay claim to such a warrant? A list, which leaves it open to an educated man to remain totally ignorant of the institutions and

history of his own country, in case he
prefers to learn an outline of the
history of Greece and Rome! Nor is
he in the whole course of his college
education under the slightest constraint
to repair this defect. Backbone an
individualistic scheme must undoubtedly get; but the existing entrance requirement is not a rational attempt to
supply one.

So much for the contents of preparatory education; by its next step the
college clips still more closely whatever
elbow-room it may have left. The student, having pursued for four years his
studies on the lines described, must
finally be put through a series of written examinations which decide his fitness to go further.[1] The question

[1] Certain institutions accept students partly or
wholly without examination, provided they are vouched
for by their secondary schools. The entrance re-

arises—how do such tests retroactively affect education?

Be it noticed that, however divergent in essence the studies, the examination form is ever the same. A specific requirement is minutely indicated: history, within such and such limits, as treated in this text book or that; geometry, to include the propositions named in an official syllabus; chemistry or physics, 40 experiments apiece, each of them set down likewise in a syllabus, which the college or the College Entrance Board distributes gratis; lit-

quirements are in these cases not less precise, but the secondary school is free to work out its own teaching and examining methods. Practically, however, the preparatory schools have not been in position to do much with this freedom, for their classes usually contain boys destined for the regular college entrance examinations, and the more definite necessities of these students dictate the spirit and method of the instruction. I must add that a decidedly more wholesome relation between high school and college exists in certain Western States.

erature, reduced to certain specified poems, essays, speeches, novels, about a dozen and a half in all. The catalogue leaves no doubt as to what the candidate must know; the examinations leave no doubt as to how he must know it. At neither point has the secondary school any option; it must identify education with passing college entrance examinations. On a sharp skirmish lasting a few hours on a hot day, the entire issue turns. A light verbal equipment, capable of being handled with agility and plausibility most effectually meets the emergency. The boy must be able rapidly to turn out categorical answers to questions framed in one way, whatever the subject matter: whether he is expounding Burke's speech, Lycidas, the binominal theorem, or the Constitution of Sulla, his salvation hangs on smooth, clear, brief formulations of pseudo-scientific aspect. Contrast this procedure with what takes place in the college: there the instructor examines his own class; nor even with this advantage is the student's passing allowed to depend altogether on the written examination. Frequently it counts only for one-third, recitation records and note-books constituting the basis of the remaining two-thirds.

Now, if in college a written examination set by the instructor himself is neither a fair nor an adequate method of appraising the value of his own students, why should it suffice in case of unknown boys under disturbing conditions? Is it not clear that the outcome will be to convert the secondary school into a cramming-machine? It would be extremely amusing to see what would happen, if the tables could be turned on the colleges; if, for instance, it were proposed to let outsiders set the college final examinations, mark the papers and award degrees on the basis of such examinations alone! Or, if graduate and professional schools should insist on going back of the Bachelor's diploma and holding rigid examinations in all the subjects in which the diploma is now assumed to be a guarantee of competency!

Two things are at once clear: first, the verbal, intellectualistic treatment which I have described annihilates natural distinctions.[1] A homely illustration will make my meaning clear.

[1] I have discussed this aspect more fully in two papers: The Preparatory School, Atlantic Monthly, September, 1904; College Entrance Examinations, Popular Science Monthly, May, 1903.

Some years ago a distinguished Professor of chemistry was said to have described to his class a cooking machine, so ingeniously contrived that in it a half-dozen or more different dishes could be simultaneously prepared. The machine worked with a single drawback; all the dishes tasted alike. This is just exactly what secondary school teaching, destined to be tested by the entrance examinations does to the varied menu that the college spreads: all the characteristic essences are cooked to death! The stimulus and nutrition that we ought to gain from variety are completely sacrificed. On their face history, literature, science, mathematics, belong to distinct categories. Into each of them a characteristic aspect of experience has been distilled; each of them is capable of touch-

ing the boy at a different angle. The
necessity of working in sharply separate fields is itself a violation of the
wholeness with which experience comes
to the child. To some extent it may be
unavoidable; but examination-necessi-
ties enormously aggravate the evil.
The damage is made irreparable when
all subjects alike are bleached and pul-
verized in the course of the intellectualistic handling entailed by examin-
ability. Mathematics lending itself so
easily to concise and consecutive formu-
lation is the model to which other subjects conform. Thus history is resolved into a succession of so-called
"facts," arranged on the shelf of
memory in tiny packages, in such wise
that the right package answers the pre-
arranged examination signal; literary
specimens are taken to pieces and

ticketed for the purpose of mechanical recall; science is a complete abstraction from natural phenomena, supposed to be re-endowed with life by exactly forty carefully designated experiments,—one more would be needless, one less, perilous.

A few typical questions will make clear just what I mean by intellectualizing studies that merit varied modes of presentation, and the sterilization that ensues:

In English,[1] for example, the candidate is asked to depict Milton's "thoughtful man"; to do which satis-

[1] The utter artificiality of the college entrance scheme comes out perhaps most strongly in its treatment of English. It proposes a program that in the matter of reading makes no distinction at all between boys and girls. The books selected, being designed for both, suit neither. The requirements in English are admirably calculated to put a summary end to the love of discursive reading on which intelligence and taste so largely depend.

factorily he must *know* rather than *appreciate* Il Penseroso, appreciation and "knowing" tending strongly to antagonize each other. A thoroughly artificial and hence futile effort is made to develop power of expression through re-vamping the contents of injudiciously chosen literary texts, instead of connecting the art of expression with the boy's vital experience outside the school room as well as inside every class in which he takes part. There is no better evidence of the unnatural way in which subjects are divorced from each other and from the boy's own life than the fact that a boy may "pass" in English, if he can retell the plot of Silas Marner, though every other paper he hands in may be close to the verge of illiteracy! In chemistry,—to look further—the candidate is more concerned to manipulate equations and formulae than to observe every-day phenomena. As mere knowing suffices, phenomena are less prominent in instruction than the generalizations "explaining" them. Finally in history, we may suppose the candidate to be called on to state the principles of the Federal party, which he will have been trained to do perfectly without the slightest consciousness that frequent dispatches from Washington now raise again the same old issue. As far as the coefficient of reality is concerned, the Federal controversy is as pale and remote as the legislation of Sulla. The boy meets the requirements in United States history without ever wetting his feet in the currents of actual life! The "successful" outcome of preparatory education turns thus on literal knowing of dead fact, not on the ability to make a varied and appropriate reaction to a living experience,—in the realms of nature, social life, politics or literature; and the coercion which fastens this kind of thing on the secondary schools and leaves them neither inducement to nor margin for intelligent procedure comes from the college.

In the light of these facts, one can understand a somewhat startling statement in a recent annual report [1] by Dean Briggs: "Of any two subjects, efficiently taught for the same length of time, one is about as good as another and deserves equal recognition in a scheme of examinations." For, clearly, when half a dozen different studies have been each purged of its characteristic essence by way of preparation for

[1] 1901–2, p. 96.

examination, then, I grant you, all being equally insipid, "one is about as good as another." But now that one thing is about as good as another, provided only it is as efficiently taught for the same length of time, why should schools be put to the trouble and expense of providing a varied diet? If all foods masticated for equal periods are equally nutritious, is not a changing, well-ordered menu a sheer extravagance? Dean Briggs argues just the other way around; if one food is about as good as another, why should a housekeeper *not* keep an abundant table? If one study is about as good as another, why should a school not provide limitless variety? But the argument is wholly fallacious. A developing civilization wants physics, philosophy, poetry. It has no way of substituting one for the other; hence, it values them alike. Pedagogically, however, their value depends on entirely different considerations. It is not simply a question of how long or how thoroughly a subject has been taught. The mere fact that Roman history and American history have been taught with equal vigor for equal school periods does not make it immaterial which a particular American boy knows. English literature and Egyptian hieroglyphics cannot be made of equal value to a high school boy by teaching them equally long with equal efficiency. There are certain studies in respect to which American society leaves the boy no option; it is impossible to substitute anything else for them, whether taught with equal efficiency or greater. There are other subjects the value of which to any individual depends almost wholly on what follows. If nothing follows, a year's or a half-year's detached study is largely a waste of time, a dissipation of energy and purpose, no matter how admirable the technique of instruction.[1] It is, I hold, impossible to speak of "efficient teaching" on a narrow basis that ignores the general conditions determining the sub-structure of education, and that fails to consider the importance to the individual of organic continuity in training. The curriculum is not, in a word, to be put together out of any elements whatsoever, provided only they measure up as equal units. A study's value cannot depend on the mere tale of the hours during

[1] This is precisely the vice of all disorganized election, as will more fully appear in the discussion of the Elective System (Chap. IV).

7   97

which the teacher has hammered and the boy squirmed! No fortuitous checker-board arrangement will meet either the general demand that society imposes on all alike or the particular purpose for which every boy is nowadays urged to keep up his education.

I insist then that the college defeats itself in advance through its narrowly intellectualistic admission machinery. Choices were introduced in order through appropriate selection to elaborate the individual on characteristic or significant lines. Now, that undertaking is, as far as the secondary school is concerned, defeated before it gets under way. The purposeful exploitation of the individual yields to a narrow, monotonous grind. Instead of utilizing a variety of resources to fructify a fertile field, the teacher must hammer away at mechanized responses. Instruction is deficient in body, volume and infectious quality. It is thin, peaked, anaemic. It leads to the examination room and there stops abruptly. Everything is done consciously and unconsciously to sound the examination motif; to discourage the enterprise, the initiative, for which the college subsequently cries aloud in vain. Let me give an example: A capable secondary school teacher, having thoroughly drilled his pupils in traversing the beaten path, might be tempted to wander with them in search of the wild flowers that shrink back from the gravelled walks. The thing is not explicitly forbidden; but, as if the teacher had not been already sufficiently controlled or the pupil sufficiently mechanized, the colleges still further emphasize the cash value of examination technique by selling former examination papers "in quantities" for use in the class-room at "ten cents a dozen." A noble employment for spare time, hardly won! Of course the pupil interprets education as synonymous with success in the fine art of passing examinations. He quickly develops a strong disinclin-ation to undertake work that does not count; he becomes a stickler for the letter of the law. He holds a stop-watch over his teacher, as the college holds one over him. How is deep-seated purpose to be brought to con-sciousness, how is peculiar power to de-fine itself, in such an atmosphere?

There is a still more weighty objec-tion to letting everything depend on rapid-fire written examinations from the outside. They act as a sieve through the meshes of which only the verbally expert readily pass. The entire transaction is in words; rather in verbal manipulations, unchecked by the severe reference to fact which can alone control and vitalize mere speech. Other types, visual, motor or what not, certainly more numerous than the purely intellectual, are severely handicapped. Contrary to the express design of modern education, their training is attempted primarily and mainly through what they are not rather than through what they are. They are penalized for what they cannot do, while the word-monger draws usury on his fluency. The boys whose processes do not readily verbalize, whose inspiration comes of contact with a genuine situation, who think in deeds rather than counterfeit thinking in words, these, the really productive types of actual life, must not only compete with the verbalist in his own field; they must translate into smooth phrases the concrete activities inserted in the curriculum in recognition of interests that do not belong to the word-game; and on the translation, not on their competency in the original, they are judged.

The one place where the actual qualities that cut a figure in life have something to do is the athletic field. There real difficulties must be met; problems in organization, discipline, adaptation of means to end, try the boy's endurance, resourcefulness and executive capacity. There intelligence, wit and energy find an outlet. The pedant who has had to take all sap out of school work surveys the animated football field and helplessly deplores the

perversity of youth. I believe the folly
of the schools to be largely responsible
for the low level at which the boy's
capacity and interests thus discharge; I
believe that a rationally conducted secondary school might successfully compete with, perhaps anticipate, the football field. At any rate the totality with
which, once given a genuine problem,
the boy throws himself upon it, is the
best answer to those who dread lest a
rational appeal to capacity means only
pandering to ease. It is exactly the
reverse; your ineffective curriculum is
called "hard," because threats and pen-
alties are together unavailing to tie the
boy's energy and attention to it. For
a fictitious "hardness" which is only the
other side of apathy and evasion, sound
educational policy would substitute
genuine difficulties, inherent in actual

situations: it would not deny to a child that stimulus of reality without which his previously "disciplined" elders will not raise a finger! Our educational— or cultural—resources are thus widened, not reduced; at the same time, an increased, not diminished, portion of the boy's energy is engaged at a high level.

The truth is that while the college has after a fashion partially modernized the preparatory school curriculum, it vetoes complete modernization of teaching ideals and methods. The curriculum once made up, the boy must submit to it; he must learn this, that and the other; and tell it in writing before proceeding further: the good old mediaeval way.

But if the psychological standpoint is valid, a very different relation has at the start to be established, as between the boy and the course of study. Consider, for a moment, what a curriculum is: each of the subjects of which it is composed is a finished abstraction from experience for the reflective satisfaction of already mature minds. Physics, chemistry, history, languages, in the shape which they assume in text books, are logical devices for the convenient analysis and arrangement of specially interesting or important aspects of experience. Meanwhile the experience itself comes to us in complex wholes. In the real world—man's and child's alike—various aspects are present in every experience. In the stone on which the boy stumps his toe, physical, chemical, geological, aesthetic facts are fused. The boy's world is emphatically this world of fused phenomena.

In the school curriculum, however, phenomena have been already broken up on logical lines. Chemistry is, for example, an affair of atoms, elements, equations, equivalences; where in the real world does the child encounter any of them?[1] Now the present preparatory school procedure largely ignores the necessity of mediation between the world in which the boy lives and that which he encounters in his text books. His actual interests abide in the former; the college cares only for the latter. A school that aims at an organic response must somewhere mediate between the two, between the crude experience of the boy and the abstract world of scientific truth. The boy must be led to find in his own experi-

[1] Notice that the college requires the boy to study chemistry *or* physics *or* some other one science!

ence the elements out of which truth and law are ultimately won; his own emotional life must illuminate the mature and reflective literary expression. Thus only can the school play a vital, as against a merely repressive or coercive part, in his development. Thus only does his education become part of his life,—the relationship which the modern school actually tries to establish. But as things are now organized, the boy's life runs in one channel; across an impassable line the curriculum runs in another. That the two are in origin identical, rather that the curriculum is a mere refinement on actual experience, never, of course, occurs to the pupil, and rarely, if ever, disturbs the teacher. From the deadly bifurcation which makes the school only an unwelcome intrusion into child life, there is no escape so long as

the academic standards of mature
scholars determine the performance of
immature boys.

I have no wish to exaggerate; the
college had undoubtedly to deal with
unsatisfactory conditions. It honestly
desired to pull the schools out of a veri-
table slough. But, unfortunately, in
its campaign for an elevated standard,
it so completely misjudged the place
for emphasis that the present condition
is in some respects more difficult, less
manageable, and no whit more satisfactory than the situation it displaced.
President Eliot has recently stated [1]
that "the American secondary schools
have distinctly lost ground within the
last twenty years." Partly this is accounted for by the athletic infection for
which, by the way, they have the close

[1] Report 1905–6, p. 46.

college connection to thank; but it cannot be wholly without significance that decay coincides exactly with the stiffening and bracing of the entrance examinations. What is one to think of the sieve that lets this deteriorated material pass through, or requires it to deteriorate thus in order to get through? What, in other words, is the meaning or value of "elevation of standard" accompanied by distinct retrogression? If the retrogression is real, the elevation can be only apparent. And such is actually the case. The standard is elevated on paper. No genuine increase of the student's power is denoted by it. No consistent or fearless effort is made to enforce it.[1]

[1] A recognized authority, who read this in manuscript comments: "Much more might be said of the false paper-standard which no college actually maintains."

THE AMERICAN COLLEGE

It is evaded in the first place by extremely considerate marking; in the second, by frequent admission with conditions;[1] and, finally, if neither of these loopholes is spacious enough, the candidate may be actually exempted from examination altogether![2]

[1] The following table shows the frequency of conditions in the entrance examinations:

College.	Year.	No. of candidates examined.	Passed in all subjects.	Conditioned in from 1 to 5 or more subjects.
Princeton	1903	412	109	303
"	1904	378	132	246
Yale	1904	422	176	246
"	1905	467	155	312
Harvard	1903	664	225	439
"	1904	710	223	487

The frequency of failure disclosed by the above figures must signify that preparatory education is on the wrong track. In mere extent, the required performance is actually far below the boy's capacity, provided this is once enlisted. The fact which the colleges wholly fail to grasp is that adolescence is wasted as long as it is treated as a mechanical college novitiate on the existing terms.

[2] This last statement does not apply to Yale and

110

COLLEGE AND SECONDARY SCHOOL

The college thus admits that the details of the preparatory education which it prescribes stand in no essential connection with what follows in the college itself. The preparatory school is forced to do one thing; the col-

Princeton, neither of which admits special students without examination. President Eliot (Report 1905–6, p. 18) quotes the Committee on Admission to the effect "that the existing system of admission by examination was too narrow and consequently inefficient" in individual cases. The Committee further (p. 342) admits "that dissatisfaction with the requirements has been constantly increasing." Its policy is to relieve particular cases by suspending the rules. To this way of curing the difficulty I object:

1. It does not really remove the stigma of failure from the boy to the system, though, by hypothesis, it is the system, not the boy, that has failed.

2. It does not restore to the boy the time, energy and educational possibilities that he had more or less to waste for four years before it was ascertained that the things he has been attempting are not really vital after all.

3. It takes no account of the damage inflicted on those that "pass." In a word, if the system is bad, it cannot be made good by special exceptions. Something much more fundamental and thorough-going is imperative.

111

lege needs something quite different. They are at cross purposes, hopelessly so, for lack of experimental opportunity within the secondary school. The novel problems raised by the necessity of dove-tailing into the elective system have been solved for—not by—the schools in advance of all experience, on the basis of easy administrative control. Thus secondary education has been through and through externalized. Our college authorities have organized centralized bureaus which are as fatal to true educational spirit and innovation as the bureaucratic educational ministries of the continent, though we have had to stop short of the protracted severity which gives the foreign schools their unique disciplinary value. Before our chains are riveted any more tightly, we might pause to reflect on this Continental experience. "Regulation goes so far that the teacher's initiative is restricted to the narrowest limits; he gets his cue not from what is here and now possible and necessary, but from some hard-and-fast ordinance, that is not rendered any more elastic or bearable by reason of the fact that it is liable to alteration at long intervals." [1] In these words, thoroughly applicable to us, Paulsen describes the bureaucratic stone wall, against which Continental reformers dash themselves in vain. The very extravagances of their propositions are to be imputed to the speculative form to which they are confined. They can do nothing; experiment is shut out. We have no governmental incubus of this sort; but we have contrived something that is rather more

[1] Paulsen, Das Deutsche Bildungswesen, p. 182.

than equivalent! In consequence the teacher of insight, initiative, originality, the teacher who wants to act upon that respect for and faith in the individual which the college professes, finds no congenial opportunity in preparatory education.

Now I submit that our education with its many unsolved problems is the last field in which this kind of organization is wise or necessary. Its need is in just the opposite direction; originality, not mechanical restriction, is required. In general, the schools are more apt to be behind than ahead of the age; more apt to hinder than to anticipate progress. Turbulent spirits do not turn school teachers; school routine does not develop revolutionists. Of all the arts, education is most liable to crystallize; and crystallization is a danger to be averted, not a tendency to be assisted, by all the pressure that the combined colleges can bring to bear.[1]

[1] Just as this book goes to press, the Fourth Annual Report of President Jordan, of Leland Stanford Jr. University, comes into my hands. It contains, with much else of great interest, an elaborate Report by a Faculty committee, dealing with the subject of this chapter. On the point just discussed the committee says: "From the first the theoretical attitude of the University has been . . . that the high school curriculum is primarily a problem for the secondary schoolmen; that the University, while lending its assistance by way of advice and insistence upon high standards should avoid all intent or appearance of dictation." And again: "It was believed that the methods and standards of work in the high school needed to be changed." And, if I may draw the obvious conclusion, such changes must largely be worked out by and within the high school. I am not, of course, urging that the high school be cut loose and left to itself. A real, inner, organic connection is to be sought, in place of the nominal, artificial bond now subsisting. If the need is best conceived from the standpoint of the college, the solution is in the same degree an experimental problem for the secondary school. But the whole force of my argument is directed against the isolation of either; complete and genuine coöperation is demanded; the situation must be comprehended as a whole. See Chap. VI "The Way Out."

115

CHAPTER IV

THE ELECTIVE SYSTEM

I HAVE shown that under present conditions within the preparatory school the battle of the elective system must be fought out almost altogether on college territory; it is thereby doomed to failure from the start. The time is inauspicious for so sudden and serious a responsibility. The construction of an educational framework, calculated to support one's subsequent activity in life, is a difficult undertaking; it means a thorough searching of the heart, a judicious weighing of interests, opportunities, abilities. Now, the secondary school training has not tested the youth's endowment; it has not matured or defined him. Can the situation of the college Freshman or Sophomore be safely relied on to induce prompt and adequate reflection? Consider the facts. Several hundred boys at the most expansive period of life, having just passed through a prolonged and odious drill, suddenly find themselves in the enjoyment of complete freedom of locomotion in an environment fairly teeming with distracting novelties. The recent preparatory school cram has not only discredited the studies actually involved in it: it has compromised mental application as such. A marked revulsion from books sets in just at the moment when the college substitutes an easily satisfied or evaded standard for the exacting daily recitation and the threatening entrance

117

examination; at the moment when academic freedom tears the youth from his moorings with a flood of fresh and exciting experiences. The student is—remember—only an American boy: his life has a thin background; he is not steadied by the traditions and conventions that in older societies keep things in place. The past does not control him; the future equally lacks fixity. Vague ambitions—his own, his family's,—hinder concentration on a definite object; well-known examples of illogical and unearned success breed a demoralizing confidence that the law of cause and effect will be suspended for his benefit, too. College life is an interlude, a respite. How can we figure out that in this moment of release from pressure, of suddenly expanded horizon, the boy may safely undertake to

118

steer his bark in unknown waters by the shifting pole-star of his own misty purpose? Until the preparatory school develops in him intelligence and conscience strong enough to control, even if not wholly to absorb him, an elective system whose outcome hangs upon the seriousness and fitness of initial choice is bound to be largely wasted and frequently abused.

The college assumes that the boy will profit by his mistakes, but it leaves him without means of correcting them. The teaching machine starts not tentatively but at full speed. A youth who after a few weeks discovers that he has mistaken either himself or his course, is powerless to set the thing right. His plight will be still worse if he switches to courses already well advanced. The opportunity and the disposition experi-

119

mentally to "taste" before committing one's self, so wisely encouraged in the German universities, are here lacking. The usual contribution towards enabling a boy to make an appropriate choice and to follow it out logically, is a class-officer or "adviser,"—a Professor with lectures to give, researches to supervise, investigations of his own to carry on. He is not as a rule qualified by his primary interests and concerns to do the delicate and tedious work of "advising"; he has no time for it. In the end it means nothing to him. As a matter of fact, intelligent advising would under the circumstances completely absorb the adviser: he would have to know all the facts at the start, and to keep them continuously in mind. Every term brings its fresh problems in selection and co-ordination; at every stage, a real adviser would have his hands full. The nominal intervention of this functionary cannot, therefore, materially affect the operation of the elective system. For the most part, advice is equivalent to perfunctory consent to propositions which the student himself submits under influences that have as a rule little to do with the avowed intention of the system.[1]

[1] A recent graduate writes me as follows: "The relations between adviser and student begin when the latter submits his schedule of studies for the adviser's approval. This operation is usually perfectly perfunctory, consumes anywhere from one to ten minutes, during which the adviser endeavors to acquaint himself with his new charge, offers a few commonplace suggestions, appends his signature and 'The deed is done.' I venture to say that in many instances here, unfortunately, the relationship between teacher and student summarily ends, never to be revived during the whole college course. I must admit that the advisory system, operated as at present, carries little weight, and I think that a large percentage of men will bear me out in the statement that it is looked upon in general as little more than a joke."

To make matters still worse, certain colleges pro-

But there are still greater difficulties ahead. What warrant can be ad-
duced from either psychology or experience for the automatic and judici-
vide a change of advisers from year to year. At
Yale, for instance, the Freshman has a class-officer
to steer him; as Sophomore, he comes under a member of the Tutorial Board; as Junior and Senior,
when his elective range is untrammeled, he is left
entirely to his own devices. All possibility of consecutive advice is thus entirely destroyed. At Cornell,
where a reaction against the elective system appears to be under way, President Schurman can-
didly states: "The need of guidance has been provéd
by experience. But in practice it has been signally
wanting. After prolonged consideration, two methods
of guidance have been adopted, one impersonal, the
other personal. Of his thirty hours, the Freshman
is required to take twelve (impersonal guidance).
At the beginning of the Junior year, the student
chooses some one Professor or Assistant Professor
as his adviser" (personal guidance). President's Report, 1905–06, pp. 25, 26, abridged. This plan is
likewise open to objection as discontinuous. The impersonal guidance of the critical Freshman and Sophomore years means no guidance at all in 3-5 of the
work; the adviser of the Junior and Senior years,
even if credited with time and interest, comes on
the field too late. His advice cannot be retroactive.
The most that he can do is to make the best of what
he finds.

122

ous self-assertion that the elective system presupposes at this particular moment? A tremendous endowment will, of course, make its way to the light; it will survive the deadly preparatory school drill. In other cases the boy's choice may or may not be significant. Who knows whether the impulse deciding the moment's choice is really more characteristic, more permanent, than the secondary interest which an intelligent instructor might develop by patiently fishing with a longer line in the deeper waters of the boy's mind?

I confess myself somewhat puzzled to make out just what it is that declares itself when the elective system abruptly gets to work, when the bars are let down and the field is opened to choice. Bent, endowment, capacity—we are told. How then is bent to be conceiv-

ed? Is it with or without premonition
of its ultimate goal, of the concrete
form in which it is destined to find em-
bodiment? Does it work as an instinct,
or as rational, self-conscious purpose?
If bent is an instinct, it must be credited with a curious affinity for appropriate college courses; for it must at
once on the basis of brief verbal desig-
nations select its proper nutriment from
some hundred pages of catalogue.
Nay, not only must it pitch upon the
course best suited to its immediate
need; it must follow this with an equally logical "next"; and so on from step
to step, until the instinctive gradually
changes into a rational process, real-
izing in its progress what in the end
turns out to be a coherent and purposeful scheme. This, on the supposition
that the Freshman's bent works itself

out after the manner of an instinct.

The alternative view assumes that the boy knows from the first what he is driving at: it makes the elective system answer a rational, not an instinctive, need. The student is now conceived as intelligently minded to be a physician, a lawyer, or an engineer. He has chosen a definite end; to simplify the case favorably for the elective system, we shall suppose him to have chosen wisely. Well, thereby he is, as far as concerns that end, estopped from further choice. His freedom is practically exhausted in that one act. To the extent to which he continues from time to time to choose freely, his original choice is likely to be thwarted or confused. For the career chosen is an objective thing for which a definite course of preparation is necessary.

There is absolutely no reason to credit a college Freshman with the seriousness or the knowledge required to put together a course of study which will in these days best serve as introduction to his vocation. Trust the boy's bent, if you will, to commit him to a proper vocation: the subsequent moves are in the main from that instant objectively determined. They cannot be left to his interest or inclination to choose from term to term. It is no longer a question as to whether he likes the indispensable preliminary steps; he likes the end; he must henceforth submit to whatever that end demands. His efficiency depends now on submission, not on assertion. To build up the groundwork required in these days for an intelligent career in medicine, law, or technical science he may be compelled to travel far from his inclination; to cultivate many repellent fields; nothing in the elective system exercises such an authoritative control over his subsidiary choices.[1] The ultimate goal once chosen, nothing compels the intervening steps to lead reasonably to it. The elective scheme has no necessary, inner logic. I may, for example, decide that my bent is medicine; and I may then prepare for a course in the medical school by wasting my time on a senseless conglomeration of Spanish, geology and fine arts; or I may utilize the same combination as a preliminary to law. A case has recent-

[1] I quote from Mr. Edmund Gosse's account of his education a sentence that covers this point: "I got the habit of going on with any piece of work I had in hand, not flagging because the interest or picturesqueness of the theme had declined, but pushing forth towards a definite goal, well-foreseen and limited beforehand."

FATHER AND SON, p. 189.

ly come to my notice in which a student, intending from the first to enter a medical school, took for four years "all the chemistry he could;" but never set foot in a class in any branch of biology!

Finally, it may be argued that the elective system need not work in either of the ways mentioned, that it need not assume either an entirely instinctive choice from step to step, or an entirely rational choice of an ultimate controlling object; in that event, I maintain, it is absolutely bound to be discursive and aimless; a thing of shreds, patches, impulses, without thoroughness, logic or coherency. All sorts of incongruous and irrelevant motives now assist in determining the student's choices, in place of the individual capacity or purpose in behalf of which the system was instituted; he takes one subject because

128

so many others take it, another because
of the lecturer, another because it has
vogue as a "culture-subject," another
because the hour is convenient, still another because it is a "snap": he must in
the supposed case choose in this capri-
cious fashion. Exclude as non-exis-
tent a sure-footed instinct, and as rare,
a clear-headed purpose, and the door
is inevitably opened to this conglomeration of impulse and influence. And
this is just what actually happens.
The most that is now claimed for the
system by its defenders is that there is
under it a "fair amount of judicious
choice of correlated subjects;" and this
they are exceedingly solicitous to dem-
onstrate. Their position is thus a curious one: there is such a thing as judicious correlation measured, of course,
by objective standards; they rejoice

9

when it is attained,—it proves that the system works and how. Yet the college has no duty towards those—the majority—whose ignorance of themselves or of the actual requirements of their probable careers, abandons them to an uncorrelated admixture of studies!

Our case is yet clearer when we pass from the immediate vocational to other aspects of individual activity. An elective system that gives effect only to dominant personal choice loses sight of other not less essential activities. Such activities are indispensably important to fulness and wholesomeness of life; they protect us against such total immersion in special occupations as would threaten to destroy the very basis of interaction among men. Now, then, neither within the college itself nor in the mandate issued to the secondary school does the college recognize the pedagogical bearing of the general conditions accompanying all forms of individual effort. It is no foregone conclusion that mere existence within a community will effectually prepare a man for his proper part in its intellectual interests and social struggles. I hold that if a liberal education is anything more than a personal indulgence or a personal opportunity, the college has a very distinct task in reference to the impersonal aspects of social and civic life.

Let me make this point clear by recourse to a concrete illustration: We will suppose a Freshman class composed of several hundred clear-headed articulate-speaking youths, each one keen, capable, knowing what he wants, resolute to do it. This is the elective system at its rarest and best: is it enough?

Not in my judgment: it amounts to sheer educational atomism; a-social, if not actually anti-social. The educated man so viewed is only an exceptionally vigorous and knowing parasite; into his hands the social and economic situation plays. It is more or less an accident, if his activity incidentally carries beneficent consequences. As far as his purpose is concerned, society is his field, his opportunity; to the extent that he is engrossed with himself, a distinct antagonism results.

It is, in a word, impossible to conceive the educational orientation of the boy as merely a matter of comfortable or advantageous professional or vocational setting. Of course, efficiency is in any case admirable; and the social value of a service is not wholly a question of its conscious intent. But it is

none the less impossible to believe that
modern intellectual life is to develop in
water-tight compartments; that the college does its full duty when it produces
separately preliminary lawyers, doctors, chemists, artists, without common
ground. In other words a man is not
exhausted, when he is trained to be engineer, doctor or mason. Such a class-
ification may be economically, it is not
socially or personally, the end of him.
It cannot, therefore, be the end of him
educationally. Society is not a mere
mosaic of sharply accentuated economic units. In the first place, relations
of immense educational importance
converge upon the individual from the
surrounding social mass. He is born
into an organized and artificial order.
His obligations are as binding as his
privileges are precious. And neither

set is obvious. Of course he adjusts himself to this social environment in a blind way as he grows up. He learns that he can vote at twenty-one; that all men are equal before the law. He absorbs the current ethical and political standards. But has higher education no positive duty here? Can it totally neglect this aspect of the boy's orientation? Under the elective system the college does neglect it; it does not require the boy necessarily to take thought of the social and civic relations here in question during a single moment of the eight years needed to get a liberal education and to lay the foundation for it. In all that immediately pertains to his calling, the college proposes to equip him at a high level, but in respect to his civic and human relations, it leaves him on the plane of accident, habit and prejudice.

In yet another respect a man's vocation does not contain him; he runs over. What we loosely call his "tastes," whether connected with what we call his business or independent of it, are equally important to the completeness of his self-expression, to his sanity and sweetness of mind. His range of appreciation must be wider than that of his express vocational activity; a supple mind is at least as important as a supple body. These facts are assuredly not without bearing on the details of an education designed thoroughly to exploit the individual. They take account, indeed, of interests that form in considerable measure the basis of large and disinterested intellectual intercourse with one's fellows; they make the broad and open highway upon which our separate and private estates open. The college attitude in reference to them is merely permissive. Opportunities are offered which would enable a student to supplement or broadly to buttress his special training. It is left altogether to chance whether he takes advantage of them. The pressure of a competition, the issue of which is decided on the narrowest lines, tends to eliminate all factors that do not count in the race. The college does nothing to resist this tendency, except through the passive offer of opportunity. Actively it even assists the tendency, by deciding fitness for its own purposes on the same narrow basis.

I submit that an education which

seeks to find for every individual his appropriate place cannot construe its undertaking narrowly without disintegrating the society it sets out to serve. It cannot survey its pedagogical problem and conceive its pedagogical procedure simply from the standpoint of the individual student,—and from a single aspect of his real concern at that. Undoubtedly its central aim is, under existing conditions to lay the philosophic and scientific foundations of typical intellectual activities. But exclusive pre-occupation with this side threatens to break up the college into several parallel, but quite separate disciplines, each engrossed in its own object. The college is, therefore, not to be regarded as a training school in the interest of bare professional com-

137

petency. It has definite functions
that go beyond the vocational destiny
of the boy.

By what token does an education
such as we have now discussed continue
to call itself "liberal"? "Liberal," if it
means anything at all, must refer to the
very elements which in the supposed
case the elective system tends strongly
to leave out of account. This is beginning to be vaguely perceived; hence an
increasingly frequent reference to "cul-
ture-courses"; a growing disposition to
explain away the aimless meanderings
of the lost elector by setting down to
"culture" what obviously cannot be
justified by intelligible purpose. Not
infrequently, I suspect, the culture motive is alleged as an apology for scholarship not high enough to support a more
serious interpretation! If, according-

ly, a student, intending to become physician, elects biology the elective system is credited with a triumph; but if a student, intending to be a banker, takes the same course, lo! there you have broad and liberal culture!

Meantime, the course in question is conducted, as we shall see in the next chapter, in explicit reference to neither: it is conducted by and for biologists! The same holds of other departments: "the teaching of mathematics under an elective system cannot comfortably take account of the non-mathematical mind," frankly admits Dean Briggs.[1] No more can—or does—the teaching of English, history, physics, or what not. An elective system in which the instructors are specialists exists for specialists. The presumption is that courses

[1] Harvard Annual Reports, 1899–1900, p. 118.

are chosen by those specially, not generally, interested in them. Of the broad fundamental concern conveyed by the term "culture," no considerable account is taken.

An effort has been made to meet this difficulty by means of a required Freshman course, which practically continues the required portion of the preparatory school routine. This procedure is supposed to contribute once and for all "breadth of culture" to the college course; and it is held to be additionally recommended by the fact that a "broad basis" is calculated to ensure the success of whatever personal superstructure is erected upon it, in the course of the three years following. Two objections may be confidently brought against this somewhat confused scheme: in the first place, "culture" thus huddled into a preliminary year takes no root,—a fact made abundantly plain by our college product; in the second, the validity of the interests here in question does not in any degree depend on their serviceableness as a basis for an education in which they are subsequently ignored. They are valid, if at all, as continuous and accompanying considerations from the very first to the very end; and not because they make a solid basis anterior to the really serious business of college education. "Culture" and "vocation" are not to be conceived as consecutive. They go along together, overlapping, playing upon each other, enriching and diversifying life as a whole, increasing its range and volume.[1]

[1] A word should perhaps be said about still another variation of the elective system. Some colleges through a guarded system of pre-requisites, others

So far I have criticized the elective system from the stand-point of principle; let us glance for a moment at its practical operation from the point of view of the students. What does it do for the seriously minded youth? What for his brother, of opposite inclination?

Of the latter we may make short work: the elective system does not exploit his capacity. It does not require him to probe himself. It simply furnishes him an abundant opportunity to

through fixed combinations or groups aim to control choice on departmental lines. These devices do not go to the root of the trouble, since they remedy none of the defects in the previous procedure. Unquestionably, however, they not only compel a certain amount of forethought, but also cut off dispersion during the years. in which they operate. In general it may be urged that while they promote departmental concentration, they fall short of both liberal and vocational organization. For this reason the modifications in question have had no great influence on the type of instruction offered, as will be shown in the next chapter exercise a low ingenuity in picking his way to a degree with the least exertion, the least inconvenience in the way of hours,[1] the least shock to the prejudices which function for him in place of ideas, tastes and convictions. He comes out at the spout as he went in at the hopper,—except for the additional moral havoc wrought by four years of "beating the game."

Capable students with well-defined aptitudes tend under the elective system to premature narrowness. They know their line; they come to college eager, capable, self-confident. Their

[1] "Young undergraduate Yale under the elective system does its best to secure courses which let it off from recitations Saturday and Monday mornings; and as absence from the single Sunday service appears to be pretty readily obtained, there is an easy possibility of two and a half days in the week of 'elective' freedom from work." Editorial, Yale Alumni Weekly, April 5, 1905.

elections hew close to their bent. There is nothing to ensure a broad basis, a large and luminous development whether from the social or vocational point of view. I have already shown how the elective system ignores the educational aspects of the inclusive social and human relationships. Further, it leaves the student entirely free to follow his special interest narrowly. Now, this amounts to anticipating in the relatively elementary stages of a pursuit, the exclusiveness that is a regrettable necessity in the very highest. It is bound to tell heavily against the solidity of subsequent scholarship. The sharp separateness of the various departments of science, for instance, is at bottom mythical. It does not exist. It is simply assumed at high levels as a matter of convenience. Of fundamental inter-relations, the elective system takes no necessary cognizance. The beginner is frequently free to take most of his courses in one department and just enough others at random to fill out his required number; and the others do not have to be cognate to any rational purpose. The prospective psychologist may thus neglect to lay in the indispensable store of physiology; the intending economist may ignore ethics and history; the historian escape adequate contact with literature or philosophy; the biologist may omit chemistry; the chemist may omit physics. The elective system impoverishes and isolates by excessive and premature specialism where it does not waste by aimless dispersion.[1]

[1] In some colleges the student is required to scatter his choices among various departments; but he

Between the two classes briefly noticed, comes the majority: the average boy, so called,—decidedly the predominant type in point of frequency. He is still to be made. Can it be seriously maintained that he clears up under the operation of the elective system, realizes what he is good for, what he is meant for? He came to college without manifest aptitude; the secondary education, which might have been a cautious effort to dissect it out or create a substitute buried it deeply under a mass of rubbish. For him, freedom means diffusion, superficiality. The elective system tempts him in a dozen different directions; arouses a dozen different interests that collapse at the moment when effort or persis-

is neither compelled nor effectively assisted to correlate these choices with each other or in reference to a definite ultimate end.

tence is demanded. This is the meaning of many isolated single courses, pursued in different departments. The elective system deteriorates into tickling of the palate. Eventually the boy's real salvation comes, if at all, when, in competition with the uneducated barbarians of the outer world, he faces the alternative of efficiency or starvation. But this is exactly what on higher ground the elective system ought to have accomplished for him. If it does not find the boy endowed with purpose, it must develop purpose within him. I do not see how the college can escape this obligation; in the end, the modern educational theory of determining the individual's destiny significantly rather than arbitrarily must be judged by the success with which we can in the interests of economy, effectiveness, variety, rely on the development in each student of high and continuous endeavor. The moment we cease to decide a boy's occupation by inheritance, convention, early and arbitrary apprenticeship, and propose, instead, to decide it by his highest capacity, that moment we are pledged to provide an intelligent and effective machinery to accomplish this object. The elective system means to be such an instrument, but it fails.

Thus far I have spoken of the elective system in its most unqualified form. The case is not essentially different in institutions that defer election until the Sophomore year and even there impose a few restrictions. Delay does not itself meet the fundamental objections to unorganized choice, superposed on a preparation that has done little or nothing to equip the boy to use such discretion. The practical effect of the postponement is merely to lengthen by a year the unintelligent preparatory school routine. At the close of the pre-scribed Freshman year, the boy is still in darkness as to the very points on which he needs enlightenment,—namely, his capacity and the special pursuits adapted to it. It is true that he has had a year in which to learn the ropes, to get acquainted through upper classmen with the character of teachers and courses; in consequence of which, how-ever, his choice is less likely to be guid-ed by his own actual needs than by col-lege gossip. In a word, when, in the Sophomore year, election begins, there is nothing to ensure even then a rational choice of studies or the intelligent correlation of studies in inter-dependent realms.

It is clear that Mr. Adams is entirely justified in objecting to the elective system as "crude, ill-considered, thoroughly unscientific and extremely mischievous." [1] Its very apologists damn it with faint praise. Harvard rests upon the modest claim that as a body the students use it with "some sense of responsibility and reasonable intelligence." [2] More recently, in replying to Mr. Adams, Prof. Hart has defended the system on the remarkable ground that it defeats itself. The objection having been urged that the student is not competent to choose from the rich banquet spread before him, Prof. Hart

[1] Phi Beta Kappa address, already quoted.
[2] Annual Reports, 1899–1900.

replies: "In practice a large number of students make most of their choices out of a comparatively small part of the offerings." [1] But does not the elective system thus desert its flag? Criticized on the ground of the student's unfitness for self-direction, it answers that as a matter of fact the student does not attempt to direct himself: he follows the pack. Prof. Hart continues: "By this process most of the good features of a fixed curriculum are actually attained, for nearly all the students choose some history, some economics, some philosophy, some science and several languages." This is a queer defence. In the beginning the fixed curriculum was set aside in favor of the elective system because it was not specifically adapted to the individual; because it

[1] Boston Transcript, June 14, 1906.

possessed no inner or organic unity. Now Prof. Hart defends the elective system by the plea that the curriculum organized by the student is just such a hodge-podge; urging that, if heterogeneity is regarded as a virtue of the old non-adjustable curriculum, the elective system is equally effective in providing a curriculum of arbitrary shreds and patches for each individual! Finally, by way of totally abandoning all pretence of actually developing the boy along vital and appropriate lines: "The usual and perhaps the best adviser of the student is the friend who recommends or warns against the courses that he has himself taken." In other words, not my own actual or probable bent or purpose, but my chum's likes or dislikes must steer me through an education established for the purposeful exploitation of my endowment! Is not this, I ask, throughout a defence of the elective system on the ground that it is not an elective system after all?

Better words than these can be spoken for elasticity. The elective system has in its present shape a negative significance only. It was a destructive attack upon an outgrown and arbitrary educational order. It performed in education the sort of service that *laissez-faire* performed in economics and politics: it battered down artificial and harmful restrictions. The educational field is now free for constructive effort: for a positive, not a negative, doctrine. It is not enough to say that the individual's maximum value depends on his finding purposeful activities and therein to assume that the necessary leading will at nineteen

153

spontaneously unroll and fulfil itself. It does no such thing; it has got to be extricated, perhaps even created, and at all events skilfully developed in all its essential external and internal bearings. This then is the sound kernel in election: the individual's bent must be heeded, if he has one; in its absence, he must be endowed with a concrete and definite object. In either case the studies employed must be combined and pursued so as to satisfy standards and requirements that exist altogether independently of the average boy's caprice. But having proposed to itself so much, the college has just begun. It cannot act as if the individual were, for educational purposes, practically exhausted by his main concern, when once this has been made out. He needs to be opened up more variously; to come in contact with his fellows at other points. He needs above all a broad and intelligent orientation in the social and intellectual as in the physical world. At various points then his interests or impulses must be extended and may be overruled. To start with, the general pre-suppositions of social and political life put a certain original compulsion upon him; later, when he has freely chosen his career, compulsion again takes place: objective standards prescribe what he is to master. The actual educational process thus always mediates between an individual of a certain significant constitution and the concrete social and physical world. The old education saw only the relative fixity of the latter; hence its dogmatic external attitude. Too often the so-called new education tries to see everything from the standpoint of individual impulse: hence its instability, its capriciousness. An organic education seeking to realize the maximum value of the individual in a given social environment will bring these two partial views together.

CHAPTER V

So far I have accounted for the inefficiency of the college by pointing out that its treatment of secondary education fails to play into the hands of the elective system, to which it leads up. I have further urged that the elective system itself at once misconceives the student and ignores the compulsory character of the correlations through which allied subjects buttress each other. Now, in the present chapter, I shall more specifically examine the teaching itself. Should still further explanation of the failure of the college vigorously to engage youth be

157

required, we shall discover it in the encroachment of graduate school methods and interests on the college department.

Historically, as I have pointed out, the expansion of the college was the acknowledgment of the equal importance of all practical activities reposing on a learned or scientific foundation, the effort to provide for each its underlying discipline. Simultaneously it became clear that these fundamental bases were not themselves fixed and finished once for all. Each of them is in the making. The chemistry that the future student of medicine requires is undergoing a continuous revision; so the physics of the engineer, the mathematics of the astronomer or logician. The moment that these studies congeal they lose part at least of their vitalizing suggestive efficacy. The stream of knowledge must keep flowing. The waters soon grow brackish, unless fed from pure, remote mountain springs. Moreover, there is no telling from what unlikely recess or dark cavern a full fresh current may be released. These considerations account for the rise of the graduate school.

The two departments are closely related; but they are not identical, nor are their needs the same. It is important for the college to keep in touch with the renovating movement just described; to welcome, test, give effect to suggestions proceeding therefrom. But its own immediate business, viewed from the standpoint of knowledge and training, is to enable the student to master the solid acquisitions that constitute at the moment the *status quo;*

to comprehend alike pre-suppositions and problems. On the resolution of these problems the graduate school later brings to bear all the formidable artillery of modern research.

Here, then, is indicated a sufficiently sharp distinction in the matter of equipment and opportunities. There is apparently no limit to the resources that advanced research may profitably employ; but the college not only does not require an equally extensive outfit,—it is bound to be injured thereby. For the necessary pre-condition to highly specialized research later is thorough preliminary training in past achievement and a more than superficial knowledge of correlated branches. It can be best obtained by means of a compact and skilfully organized curriculum, adequately taught amid conditions in which the teacher and his pupil are in close and constant intercourse. Such training is an abundant occupation for an ordinary college course; and it is likely to be seriously interfered with by the tempting proffer of opportunities that really belong to the graduate school.

The proper work of the graduate school then rests upon a definite college foundation, just exactly as, each in its peculiar way, the study of law or medicine rests upon it. With a view to every one of them, the college is to develop the boy's power, harden his fibre, put an edge on his purpose, and inculcate a usable basis of fundamental knowledge. With amazing blindness to the necessary chronological relationship according to which one of these functions must precede the other, the American college practically amalgamates the undergraduate and graduate departments! The college becomes thus practically coextensive with the graduate school. It covers an equally wide territory and in just as great detail; necessarily to the prejudice of its own essential function.

The amalgamation is of course not avowed. Ostensibly the two departments are distinct. They profess quite different objects; they confer different degrees; they are controlled by separately organized boards; they are even described in different pamphlets. But, astonishing to relate, in all that actually constitutes a school, namely, in the instruction offered, the college and the graduate department are practically identical!

This then is the situation: the Ameri-

can university offers certain lecture and
laboratory courses and exercises; first,
it labels them the college and opens
them to boys fresh from the secondary school in quest of the Bachel-
or's degree; next, it labels them graduate school, and opens them at the same
time to mature men, engaged in win-
ning the Doctorate! In a vast majority of university exercises, graduates
and undergraduates mingle; despite
different antecedents and different
aims, at the close of each course, every
student is supposed to have got what is
appropriate to his wants and needs.
Two or three targets stand side by side;
with one bullet the instructor undertakes to hit the bull's eye in each.

The courses in question usually fall
into three classes, according to the needs
of the students to whom they are sup-

posedly best adapted: those primarily intended for undergraduates, those primarily intended for graduates, and those intended in equal measure for both. Practically nowhere does the word "exclusively" appear.[1] The old class distinctions have also almost entirely vanished. Even where they are retained, a course is often announced as equally suitable to "sophomores, juniors and seniors," and graduates are not excluded. It is thus designed to gather in the same classes undergraduates at almost every stage of advancement, and no precaution is taken against still further complicating the situation for the instructor by allowing graduates also

[1] Princeton, just fairly started in developing a graduate department, announces that its graduate courses "are open to graduate students only." It does not close undergraduate courses to graduate students.

freely to filter in. Nothing can be called strictly graduate or strictly undergraduate. In the most advanced
courses, there is no assured privacy for
maturity or competency. In one institution the consent of the instructor
opens certain specifically graduate
courses to undergraduate students; in
another, it is "the object of the new arrangement to lead the undergraduate
to feel that under the elective system, he
has the great opportunity of doing in
college, at least some one piece of advanced work." So the "unripe" undergraduate invades the seminaries and
research laboratories, just as the ripe or
over-ripe graduate straggles into the
introductory courses. Under such conditions, no really scholarly tests regu-
late admission to advanced opportunities. Wherever the undergraduate's

entrance to courses, primarily intended for graduates, depends merely upon the informal consent of the instructor, the temperament of the instructor, rather than the scholarship of the student, is put on trial. It is impossible to regard this formality as constituting an effective bar to incompetency and immaturity.

As against this tendency to compound an emulsion of graduate and undergraduate students of all stages, I maintain that radical differences in age, attitude and aim cannot be ignored. The graduate student is physically and mentally grown; the undergraduate is physically and mentally growing. The former has the seriousness of maturity; the latter, the flightiness of youth. The graduate has his eye on a career; the undergraduate is still beating about in search—or avoidance—of one. The graduate has wants; the undergraduate has chiefly needs. The college is trying to make something of the boy—a scientist, for instance; the graduate school is trying to make science. How can a single class exercise at one and the same time serve ends so disparate? Of course, the graduate school does not merely investigate: the critical study of achieved results is prominent. Likewise the college gets far beyond the shallow water in which it pushes off. But the two do not therefore meet. If the B. A. degree signifies anything, the graduate student, who is going ahead on his elective line, must have already traversed, wholly or largely, even the deepest water which the undergraduate attempts; at the very least, the pace of the elder should be swifter.

Further, the two departments and hence the instructors in every classroom are subject to diverse kinds of responsibility; they regard their students from sharply contrasted points of view. Practically the dividing line must perhaps be somewhat arbitrarily drawn, for the boy merges imperceptibly into the man. But the distinction is none the less real and important; the hazy border between two patches of color does not make the patches themselves hazy. The college never loses sight of the boy as boy; he is to be initiated into studies that must be employed to reach and to stimulate his intelligence. Now, as opposed to this personal concern, the graduate school

168

is uncompromisingly objective. It is indifferent to individuals. Its heart is set on the outer fact. And for the outer fact no price is too great to pay. An exacting technique, pitiless and disinterested, eliminates personal considerations; the severity of science and scholarship knows no mitigation: their standards are brutally careless of the worker. How different the college atmosphere, where the strictest standard is satisfied to accomplish with the student the best it can,—his inheritance, endowment, environment considered!

The experience of the Harvard Law School illustrates the point I am making. Formerly college undergraduates were permitted to take work in the law school, and men registered in the law school were permitted to complete unfinished college work. The practice

169

has been discontinued, because carefully prepared statistics show that such students fall far below the men whose work is solely in the law school and whose interests are solely in graduate work. Do the highly specialized pursuits of the Graduate School of Arts and Sciences require less maturity than the study of law?

It is true that the instructor is vested with power to exclude the unfit. The authority is bound to be amiably exercised; for vigorous action would at once effect the separation which the present system is designed to avoid. In consequence instruction does not sharply define itself. It is, within a single course, elementary and advanced by turns; oscillating, according as the instructor is at the moment the more keenly conscious of one or the other component of his double audience.

Effective instruction, however, presupposes a homogeneous assembly. The good teacher cannot deliver himself into the air; his utterance takes form in direct reference to his hearers. A Berlin professor, discussing university co-education on the Continent, objected that the frequent admission of women whose preliminary training had rarely been sufficiently thorough, necessarily impaired the homogeneity of the student body, without which no lecturer can keep to a uniform level. I recall a very clear illustration to the same effect in a college exercise in economics that I once witnessed. The course belonged to the second division; it was thus stamped as equally suitable to both graduates and undergraduates. The instructor was thoroughly

171

admirable,—keen, vigorous, scholarly. He questioned closely, alertly, but always fairly, with the obvious purpose of compelling the student to see the point at issue in the light of fundamental principle. But every effort to go ahead with the maturer minds was frustrated by the recurring necessity of stating and expounding the elementary principles from which the discussion ought to have promptly pulled away. The exercise was thus confused and futile, despite the brilliancy and energy of the instructor, who, at its close, himself made to me two significant comments: that some of the best men in the class were absent,— conclusive evidence that the instructor's right to exclude the incompetent does not secure a homogeneous class; and that the course ought to be made more difficult of access by being placed in the third division—an admission of the impossibility of addressing graduates and undergraduates on even terms.

In the chaos which I have described all interests suffer; but on the whole, the graduate school gets the better of the college. It is inevitable that the more recent, vigorous, and clear-sighted department should encroach. The college is not sure of itself; the graduate department knows just what it wants. Hence graduate interests, ideals, methods have tended to prevail; and resources accumulated in the first place for the prosaic purpose of training boys have been diverted through uncongenial methods to alien ends.

For the graduate schools have as a

rule no separate funds or endowments.[1]
They are supported out of the general
or college income. Now the extent to
which the college income has been thus
withdrawn from its historic object no
one knows, not even the institutions
themselves.[2] Graduate instruction is
obviously expensive. Man for man it
costs far more to train a research
worker than an undergraduate.[3] The
college resources are not adequate to

[1] The recently established Harvard Graduate School
of Business is an exception; but in general the statement in the text holds.

[2] The annual Reports of the Treasurers make no
attempt to apportion expenditure as between undergraduate and graduate departments. Appealing to
the Treasurers or Presidents themselves for more
definite information, I have been told that the ac-
counts cannot be separated.

[3] The Report of the Treasurer of Yale University
(1906–07) gives (p. 11) the average cost per student
in the graduate department as $79.34, in the un-
dergraduate as $326.10. This appears to contradict
my statement. But the detailed statement (p. 65)
shows that in the estimate of the cost of graduate

174

both demands; it is highly question-
able whether they actually suffice for
either. A conflict of interests thus inevitably arose. It was in this situation
important to proceed cautiously and
with open eyes: to decide on educational grounds the order in which com-
peting claims should be met. It was,
in a word, necessary to count the cost.
But the cost could hardly be counted in
advance and has not been counted yet.
Incredible as it may seem, such is at
this moment the case. No American
university knows to-day, even approxi-
mately, what it expends in salaries, laboratory expenses, materials, appa-

instruction, the items admitted are only "administration, clerical work, printing, postage, remission of
tuition" etc. The entire expenditure for salaries,
laboratories, etc., for both graduate and academic
(undergraduate) departments is charged to the latter. These figures therefore throw no light on the
topic under discussion.

ratus, books for its graduate instruction, despite the fact that the interest of the graduate school is at many, perhaps most, points, distinct from that of the college. The whole subject, inevitably involving the efficiency of college training, is involved in darkness and confusion. The American university is in the plight of a general who has divided his forces without knowing exactly how. The one thing that may be confidently asserted is this: that through the expansion of graduate instruction, the college has drifted into a policy which with existing resources necessarily carries with it the inefficiency of much undergraduate instruction.[1] We shall see in a moment the

[1] In the Report previously referred to, President Jordan says: "Thus far in America, the one has antagonized the other. There has been a tendency

176

GRADUATE AND UNDERGRADUATE

make-shifts and stop-gaps with which the undergraduate is at the critical point of his training required to put up; the severe, international tests to which research is fortunately exposed forbid trifling in that region. For that the most competent teachers must be secured, the most delicate and recent apparatus, the best material, the latest literature; the institution that once embarks on research is committed to a relatively high and increasing scale of expenditure. If a single tiller is open to both parties in interest, there is no question as to which will dip more deeply into it.

I am not unmindful of the fact that to some extent college and graduate school stand on the same footing.[1]

to build up the university work by neglect of the collegiate work." p. 19.

[1] I have already (p. 48, note) conceded that in

12   177

This is true of all endowments given for general purposes since the establishment of graduate departments. But an equitable portion of the income from these sources, supplemented by gifts expressly made for advanced work is still far from covering the cur-

certain institutions (Johns Hopkins, etc.) the graduate and undergraduate departments are historically in this position. But it is still possible to question the wisdom of dividing their resources. On this point, President Pritchett, of the Carnegie Foundation for The Advancement of Teaching says with great force in the Report from which I have already quoted: "Whatever may be the advantages of the combination of the college and the university into one organization, I am convinced that it would be of immense value to the educational system of the country if a few strong universities could be established, with generous facilities for social intercourse, but without undergraduate colleges. Such institutions would, if properly endowed and supported, constitute an independent influence in the formation of university standards which could not fail to benefit all universities alike. It is to be regretted that some of the newly founded institutions did not forego the prestige of an undergraduate college for the sake of this leadership." p. 95.

rent expenditure for graduate interests. As for the rest, the policy of the university can be vindicated only if the proximity of a graduate department is absolutely essential to the vigor of the college. The independent importance of research constitutes of itself no valid excuse for a partial abandonment by the college of its historic and still necessary function. Our universities have in general assumed that whatever promoted the interest of the graduate school promoted in equal measure the interest of the college. This was a dangerous assumption. It is still unproved.[1] I shall endeavor to

[1] I may again quote from President Pritchett's Report: "Whether the amalgamation of the college and the university into a single organization bearing the name of university is the wisest solution of the type of American institution of higher learning or not, it will be admitted that this action has tended to still further confuse in the minds of the public

show in some detail how disastrous have been its consequences to the college proper.

I have said that graduate ideals and interests have tended to prevail in partnership affairs. This deference to the graduate interest begins with the organization of the faculty. The two departments—graduate and undergraduate—possess a single faculty. Original appointments are usually made to subordinate positions; promotion is by merit. Whether this plan will inure to the benefit of the college side or that of the graduate side— it cannot inure to their benefit equally, —depends wholly on the meaning of merit. As a matter of fact heavy odds

the distinction between the college and the university, or at least to obscure the fact that the university, as at present organized, has *two entirely different functions."* p. 95. (Italics mine.)

favor the graduate interest. The thing works out thus: A large number of instructors must be appointed in the first place for undergraduate service. This body is the nursery out of which through successive stages professorial material is selected. Clearly the prospect of a man's developing to professorial proportions will figure largely in determining his appointment to an instructorship; likewise within the body of instructors, promotion will fall to those who give quickest and clearest evidence of such development. The plan is a good one, only if the requirements of a college instructorship coincide with the incipient symptoms of professorial competency. If the two make different demands, then the immediate needs of the one cannot be best satisfied by selections that look chiefly to the ultimate requirements of the other.

Now, according to prevailing ideals, the supreme desideratum in a graduate school professor is capacity to carry on and inspire research. Mere teaching ability is not of course despised; but it is not enough, it is not even indispensable. On the merit plan, therefore, subordinate positions afford the means of assembling and trying out research talent. A mere teacher may indeed become an instructor; he will also remain one. Promotions every where go to promising specialists and investigators.[1]

[1] President Hadley (Report 1906) explains Yale's policy in reference to the Junior instructor as follows: "If we keep places free at the top, we increase his opportunity for promotion, if his discoveries turn out as he expects." No mention is made of the possibility of promotion on any other basis than that of discovery. The effect of this on the

GRADUATE AND UNDERGRADUATE

I confess that I see no way to avoid this policy, if a single faculty is at one and the same time to serve the two departments; my point is that it insidiously sacrifices the college. Absorption in laborious investigation, on which the future of the instructor depends, is calculated to abate the appetite for routine college teaching. Hence it happens that a college instructor is commissioned to teach boys by reason of a proficiency and interest that frequently unfit him to do that very thing; by reason of a promise whose fulfil-

quality of the teaching is obvious. It is elsewhere assumed in the same report that "teaching and discovery are both done at their best when done in combination." But no one has yet explained why the minute investigations of the modern specialist, fighting in close quarters for scientific or linguistic detail and consequent promotion, constitute him at that same moment, the best possible teacher of young students, learning and applying general principles. There seems to me a distinct antagonism involving both the time and the interest of the investigator.

183

ment will be balked, if he devotes himself whole-heartedly to the work he is ostensibly appointed to do.

I do not undervalue research; I am simply trying to point out that it sets up its own conditions and that they are by no means always or necessarily those that prevail in the region just below. Research is a highly specialized activity which for its own sake ought to be carefully reserved to students qualified by previous training and actual ability. Were I at this moment discussing the graduate school rather than the college, I could illustrate the folly of loading down gifted and promising investigators with an exhausting and distasteful college routine. It seems to me nothing short of absurd to hold that every boy at college ought to be stimulated to do "advanced work." His time and energy do not suffice for his proper college duty. His one piece of research means a scrappy addition to an already overburdened literature by one who cannot thoroughly know what has been previously done or the actual bearings of what he is supposed to be about. Surely for the sake of his single dubious contribution to knowledge it is not worth while to select his teachers according to graduate school standards.

The marks of a properly qualified college teacher are, on the other hand, quite distinctive: he must be a broadly trained and broadly minded scholar, not necessarily a first-hand investigator: a purveyor, rehandler, relator, rather than a discoverer. His interest would usually lie in incorporating newly ascertained facts in their connections, in correlating, interpreting, interrelating data and principles within and between various realms: scope, sympathy, an active pedagogical concern should distinguish him. Capacity of this kind is not invariably associated with the intense and usually narrow bent that gives to modern research its peculiarly fleshless character. For example: one type of man is well fitted to teach boys French: to open up to them what is stimulating, suggestive, engaging in French literature. A totally different type of being delights in French phonetics, obscure French dialects, etc. The fact that a man burns to do the latter, is an excellent reason for excusing him from doing the former. Once recognize the differentiation and we cease to lament that the burden of college routine in-

terferes with the professor's original
work: of course it does; it ought! So
does the practice of medicine interfere
with a man's cultivation of medical research, so does engineering interfere
with speculation in the domain of elec-
trical theory. College teaching is a
practical enterprise, not a side-issue:
men engaging in it make a choice.
They do one thing; they forego another. Very justly they complain if
they are too busy to keep up with what
is going on. So too, the physician,
who is too busy to read his journals, has
a grievance. The assimilative must
come in contact with the investigative
activity; to some slight extent they may
overlap. But an effective college cannot be organized on the supposition
that they coincide.

As a matter of fact, the qualities of

the college teacher are far more likely to protrude in the secondary than in the graduate school. Indeed, no single move will go farther towards putting college and secondary school on proper terms with each other and towards impregnating both with real pedagogical interest, than recognition of this fact; from tried secondary school men of broad and progressive scholarship, the college faculty ought to be in part recruited. Secondary school teaching is now a blind alley; it ought to be made the avenue to collegiate preferment. We should then get secondary school teachers upon whom the door of hope had not closed,—a wholesome thing for them—and college teachers whose position does not mainly depend upon doing well something that lies on the far side of their daily duty;—a whole-

188

some thing for their pupils. Of
course, one occasionally finds in a college faculty men who have taught in
the secondary schools. But with very
few exceptions they did not get their
college appointments on the basis of
their secondary school experience; they
had first to get over that, by enlisting
in the graduate student army and establishing some presumption of talent
for research!

The assimilation of the college to
the graduate school, once fairly started
in the ways described, travels forward
rapidly. "Academic freedom" is the
slogan of investigation. The college
soon becomes as "academically free" as
the graduate school. For instance, a
newly-made Doctor whose personal for-
tune and interest lie elsewhere is appointed to teach college boys; in the

189

name of academic freedom he is turned loose in the classroom to "apply his own theories and to follow his own bent."[1] He teaches what and "as he thinks fit!"[2] As a result much of the instruction given to undergraduates is far too highly specialized in content and method of presentation to be adapted to any but expert use. This difficulty has been recognized at Harvard; it cannot be remedied except by a thoroughgoing reorganization. The committee from whose report I have quoted says with unconscious irony that the method of instruction described "has helped to make Harvard College what it is." Is it not incredible that such haphazard procedure should be seriously put for-

[1] Report of Committee on Instruction in Harvard College, p. 11.
[2] President Hadley expresses a similar view, Report, 1906, p. 10.

ward as sound pedagogy? We are speaking of boys, whose work must be organized. Every step ought to lead somewhere; every course is supposed to be material to the boy's purpose. Can the individual instructor be left free to take such account of these facts as he pleases, whether in the substance offered or in the method pursued? The subject's bent, the boy's bent, enter the calculation; the instructor's bent has little or nothing to do with it. The college, academically free, thinks otherwise. Every course stands on its own bottom; the novice follows his star. It is no part of the business of the department head closely to organize undergraduate instruction, to co-ordinate courses, to impose standards. His intrusion is resented: the instructor's classroom is his castle! "The present methods of instruction are in some measure determined by department policy or are at least in general agreement with the ideas of the various departments!" [1] "In some measure, at least in general agreement," these phrases sum up the degree of co-operation within a department, and the degree of guidance on which the novice may count. The unhampered sweep that belongs to the investigator is thus conferred upon the instructor who ought to have a definite task to do, and who ought to be held to strict accountability for the way in which it is done. A college instructor in English, frankly confessing himself appalled by the difficulties he encountered, told me recently that no superior officer of his department had ever set foot in his class-

[1] Ibid, p. 10.

room, that he knew only in a general way what other men were doing with the problems with which he was contending,—that he was, in a word, academically free to do what he could or would!

We are in position now to comprehend the vogue of the lecture system. It marks one step further in the assimilation of the college to the graduate school. By it the last shackle is struck from the college student; thenceforth he is in possession of unabridged academic freedom. For the lecture system—most unqualified in the large preliminary courses—totally destroys all contact between student and teacher at that critical moment when the schoolboy becomes a college man. There is of course another obvious consideration at work. The colleges are either overcrowded or have spent in other ways the means that are needed to provide thorough fundamental teaching. It may, I think, be safely affirmed that, if thorough fundamental teaching were provided in place of huge inexpensive and ineffective general lecture courses, the shifting of emphasis together with the financial outlay involved would bring about an immediate and far-reaching reorganization: so true is it that advanced work and the graduate school have developed, not on the basis of, but at the expense of, thorough preliminary collegiate work. The lecture system, however, permits the college to handle cheaply by wholesale otherwise unmanageable numbers. The lecturer presents the subject; it is immaterial to how many, so long as his voice fills the auditorium. Relieved of the necessity of ascertaining how far ideas are assimilated, he preserves a portion of his time at least for the work on which his standing in the world of scholarship and thus in the university depends.

I do not deny that as a method of teaching the lecture has its uses. It is unsurpassable as a method of orienting trained and competent workers in an extensive field. There is no better way to depict the internal structure, the outer connections, of a subject at large. So it is employed in the German universities; so it would find a place in the final stages of the college and in the graduate school. Give a trained student just such direction, suggestion, stimulus, and he is off. But premature, general and indiscrim-

195

inate lecturing defeats the formation of the very habits on which successful lecturing presumes.

The lecture is also well adapted to Lyceum duty. There its main purpose is to lift up heads that the day's work bends too inflexibly over the craftsman's bench or the accountant's desk, in order that a man's eyes may traverse the sky or note the changing objects on the distant horizon line. Impressionability, not scholarship, is sought. Doubtless there are realms to which even college boys are best introduced in this way,—but, assuredly, not thus is the foundation of their lifework to be laid.

The general lecture courses on which the entire superstructure is expected to rest are fairly characterized as Lyceum courses. They are given by eminent men; they are immensely entertaining, authoritative, at times stimulating. It is a thrilling experience to hear brilliant men sketch a science in bold, quick outlines. But is it good elementary teaching? Does the boy carry away what he needs? Does he get precise notions? Is he compelled to think closely? The thing is too general, too irresponsible.

Once more, an astonishing failure in pedagogic insight! The mature, settled graduate student is in the laboratory and seminary in constant contact with his teacher. He is at every turn accountable; he is mercilessly criticized, he is required to define and defend himself, to try conclusions with a kindly but inexorable master. The lines are tightly held: vagueness, inaccuracy are exposed; thoroughness, clearness secured; indolence, ignorance, misapprehension get short shrift. If such procedure is wholesome and necessary to mature minds, what considerations make it superfluous for ignorant and loosely-jointed boys?

For all practical purposes the American college keeps the professor at arm's length from the beginner; in the more advanced college work, the lectures are somewhat less formal and are at times interrupted by quizzing of a kind. But the lack of painstaking grounding in the rudiments, and the common absence of preparation for the day's specific business, go far to render the attempt to quiz quite futile.

The introductory courses seem to me, therefore, to furnish the key to this situation. To them the boy's slipshod conceptions go back; they habituate him at the outset to passivity and procrastination. From this collapse, the college usually seeks an escape through a system of assistantships: let us observe its operation and outcome.[1]

Briefly put, the lecturer lectures, assigns subjects for occasional written theses and sets monthly and half-yearly examinations; the assistant reads and grades the themes and the examination papers; besides, once a month he meets the students individually for ten or fifteen minutes to "talk over their reading with them, and assists them by explanation, advice and suggestion."[2]

[1] What I have said of the excessive prevalence of lectures applies quite commonly to small as well as large institutions. Increasing use of lectures is felt to mark a college as "grown-up." The extent to which assistants are employed and the scope given to them is largely a question of the size of classes. There is less uniformity in this matter than anywhere else. The type discussed in the text is, of course, confined to some of the most populous institutions.

[2] Report of Harvard Com. on Improve. Instruct. pp. 6, 7.

The teacher has thus no necessary communication with his auditors. To him the class is an undifferentiated mass. He has no effective way of knowing whether his words tell, who works, who shirks. He gets no illumination from theses and examination papers: he never sees either!

The actual teachers, the men with the responsibility to see that the boy understands and does are the assistants: who then are they?[1]

It is difficult to characterize them in general terms, for they form a motley group. They are for the most part meritorious g r a d u a t e students— "Young and therefore without much experience in teaching"[2]—who are

[1] Sometimes the lecturing Professor is eliminated; and the fundamental teaching is wholly in the hands of assistants of the type described.

[2] Report of Com. on Improv. Instr., pp. 6, 7.

earning their way as research workers by sacrificing a few hours weekly to other uses. Not infrequently an assistantship is bestowed in order to enable a man to continue his pilgrimage to the Ph.D. degree; often, the assistant is a Ph.D. of recent origin—a fledgling not quite ready to fly or without a place to fly to. Two features stand out: the transitoriness of the body, its absorption in graduate aims. Can a changing body of more or less inexperienced young men, with no real stake attached to the performance of a perfunctory and underpaid incidental occupation, each of them simultaneously busy upon really congenial tasks to which a twenty-four hour day is at best inadequate,—can a body so constituted, I ask, effectively mediate between the lecturer and his class? I am exceed-

ingly anxious to be fair to the assistant,
however severely I comment on the system; but my impression is that they
regard their duties as an interruption,
—a deplorable, unavoidable interruption, doomed to futility at that.

Let us follow the working of this
system in a concrete case.[1] The subject will probably be entirely new to
the freshman, and certainly not easy.
For a general outline of the entire field
—the basis on which all subsequent
work rests—the college provides a
course of lectures given three times
weekly for a half-year: forty or fifty
lectures distributed over some three

[1] I discuss here the Harvard method of employing
assistants; other methods are in vogue at other large
institutions. But the particular method is of little
consequence. The entire practice of delegating important fundamental teaching to hard-pressed students working for advanced degrees is, in my judgment, indefensible.

months. The lecturer suggests the use of a general handbook to accompany the course,—he does not, however, follow closely its order or adhere strictly to its views; from time to time more definite recommendations as to additional reading are made for the elucidation of special points. Now then, all that the college does to make sure that the boy can do and is doing his work is once a month to give him a ten or fifteen minute interview with an assistant of the qualifications just described! During this month something like one-third of the whole field has been traversed in the lectures; the essential basic facts, concepts and problems stated and discussed; at its close an assistant meets the beginner for a quarter of an hour to test his knowledge, explain away his difficulties, and direct his stumbling footsteps for the next thirty days! Not a single lecture but raised more difficulties than can be cleared up intelligently in the time allotted to the crop of an entire month!

Occasionally the work is somewhat differently organized. Lectures are given only twice weekly. In the third hour, an assistant meets a section of some thirty or forty students, so selected that each student attends one such meeting monthly. But neither arrangement is intimate enough to be efficient. A good teacher of boys in a fundamental course must have his hand on his pupil's pulse; no lecturer can hear answers through an assistant's ears or read theses through an assistant's eyes. Finally, the time allowance is frankly ridiculous,—call it fifteen minutes monthly for each boy, or fifty

GRADUATE AND UNDERGRADUATE

minutes monthly for a section of forty.
The most expert assistant cannot break
ground in such conditions. I know an
assistant who, utterly desperate, con-
fers in writing. He sets a few simple
questions, having answered which the
boy departs. The fact is that the ice is
thin and one must skate warily. The
assistants cannot afford by fearless
quizzing, to expose the shallowness and
superficiality in which such instruction
necessarily eventuates; they cannot, by
applying strict standards, permit the
students to throw the responsibility
where it belongs. The standard is thus
necessarily low.[1]

Naturally enough, these conditions

[1] The passing mark is usually 50% and the marking is, as a rule, lenient. The Harvard committee
already quoted admits that the amount of study in
the undergraduate department is "discreditably
small."

put an end to systematic study. The professor does not know what is going on; the transient youthful instructor who represents him lacks compelling authority. There is thus no pretence that the student keeps pace with the lecturer by concurrent reading or studying. As a rule, lecture notes and required reading silently accumulate until an imminent conference or examination looms on the horizon. Then there is a vigorous rattling of dry bones; a sudden flare of energy; a hasty session with an expert crammer; a quick skirmish with books of reference. A well-known professor told me that he entered the faculty resolved to break up this practice. He determined to quiz his students for a few moments at every meeting on the subject of the previous lecture before going on to develop it further.   Surely, an eminently sensible procedure.   Well, he was unable to persevere.   The current was too strong for him.   Only concerted and fearless action on the part of the entire faculty could carry through so radical a departure, and of such action there was no hope.   It continues generally impossible to require college students even to read their notes between lectures.   Plainly a loss of dignity, a return to the outgrown ways of the secondary school is involved in "studying one's lessons!"

Quite recently Princeton has won honorable distinction through an independent experiment in this field.   In each of several departments, preceptors or tutors have been put in charge of small groups, with whom they meet informally and intimately.   The tutor is

not, however, expected to go over the
ground covered by the professor in his
lectures. The tutor's work rather sup-
plements or illustrates the general lectures. The professor thus continues
to expound principles which, in that
form, the boy may, or may not, grasp.
The tutor, without any direct responsibility on this score, reads with his small
group additional or illustrative material. Unquestionably the tutors do on
this arrangement enjoy a genuine pedagogical opportunity. But I cannot
see that the system offers any assurance
of a sound or adequate sub-structure.
The professor's lectures must still be
regarded as the backbone of the departmental work, and only the examination
determines whether the student has
properly apprehended them. If not,

it is then too late to do anything but register his failure.[1]

Decided sagacity has been displayed in some institutions by the students in perfecting their own machine. The logic of the thing runs thus: Survival is essentially a question of passing a regular succession of examinations. No concurrent preparation of work is required; no tests are sprung. An easy standard acquits the student who has paid with decent regularity the perfunctory tribute of attendance at

[1] I should add that the preceptor ranks decidedly higher than the assistant in dignity and salary; his grade is practically equivalent to that of assistant professor. The reader will find the aims and operation of the system discussed in President Wilson's recent reports. It is claimed that it has already effected a marked improvement in the attitude of the student in respect to his work. It will be interesting to observe how the attitude and efforts of the preceptors are affected by the growth of Princeton's graduate school.

14 209

lectures. Now, in periods varying from a single hour to several days, an expert tutor can train almost any sort of student to clear the barriers; the process is entirely mechanical. Experts in this line will undertake to train a color-blind man to pass the railroad color tests without in the least actually improving his defective color sense!

This industry is mainly concentrated in the hands of a small group of keen business men, not overladen with either scruples or scholarship. They take into their service on commission as many graduate students as the traffic requires. Here at least is a teaching staff, running parallel with the college catalogue. The business has grown to enormous proportions. A few years ago an instructor who described himself "as having gone every gait at college" assured me that in his college thousands upon thousands of dollars change hands annually in the course of this illicit commerce; that no small part of it comes from students whose "necessary" expenses are met by painful sacrifices at home. The methods employed are explicitly adapted to the immediate ends for which the service is sought:—the adroit and painless administration of minimum doses of predigested lore. Through personal attendance on the lectures or through an agent, the tutor gets possession of the material. He casts it into easily assimilable shape; danger and the boy's genuine absorptive capacity—which the college persistently underrates—do the rest. Nor does the trade confine itself to "talking" subjects—literature, philosophy, government, in which fluency,

211

self-possession and a fact or two may make a brave show. I have met successful instances of this death-bed treatment in highly technical courses:—cryptogamic botany, musical theory, and physics, in some of which a highly intricate terminology learnt for the first time the night before examination weathered a final three hour test next day. The lecturers themselves rarely appreciate the extent to which fraud and evasion flourish; but the assistants who read the papers mark the suspicious sameness of the waters that flow from one tutorial font. For the helplessness of the college in this situation, the fatal division of authority between lecturer and assistant is primarily responsible.

Before leaving this subject, I must

make it plain that I am condemning a
system, not men: the efforts of the
teaching staff to work an unworkable
machine, though unavailing, are unre-
mitting. They are caught between
absolutely inconsistent necessities.
They can neither teach deliberately nor
investigate composedly. The system
is hard on the boys, it is tragic for the
men who must administer it. They are
both overworked and underpaid.[1] For
the love of learning they have fore-
sworn worldly careers, with all the sacrifices for themselves and their families
therein involved. And now in lieu of

[1] The financial status of the American professor
and instructor is exhaustively set forth and most
luminously discussed in Bulletin Number Two of
the Carnegie Foundation for the Advancement of
Teaching. I regret that its publication comes too
late to permit me to profit by its contents; the
facts that it assembles and interprets throw a flood
of light on the problems of university organization.

the opportunity they sought they must accept a wretched compromise, equally fatal to good teaching and to unfetter- ed research.

CHAPTER VI

THE WAY OUT

MY position thus far may be briefly summarized as follows: The American college is wisely committed to a broad and flexible scheme of higher education through which each individual may hope to procure the training best calculated to realize his maximum effectiveness. The scheme fails for lack of sufficient insight: in the first place, because the preparatory school routine devised by the college suppresses just what the college assumes that it will develop; in the second place, because of the chaotic condition of the college curriculum; finally, because research has largely appropriated the resources of the college, substituting the methods and interest of highly specialized investigation for the larger objects of college teaching.

The way out lies, as I see it, through the vigorous reassertion of the priority of the college as such. The point of emphasis must be shifted back. There is the meat of the whole problem. Historically Yale, Columbia, Harvard, Princeton are colleges. The B. A., not the Ph.D. is, and has always been, the college man. The college has been richly endowed. And it is the college, where a boy may be trained in seriousness of interest and mastery of power, that the nation pre-eminently needs. The graduate school is a late development: a proper beneficiary of the college surplus, if such there be, not the legitimate appropriator of the lion's share of its revenues.

I mean neither to depreciate nor to disparage graduate work; to the extent of advocating a more exclusive treatment of its privileges, a more thorough fitness for its opportunities, I am doing just the reverse. But I insist that rapidly won distinction as research centres is no compensation for college failure. The diversion of college resources to graduate uses is defensible on the theory that college work is antiquated or superfluous: but this plea can hardly be urged, at a time when the graduate schools themselves suffer from slighted college work. Its neglect of its primary duty in favor of wider adventure subjects the college to exactly the same criticism and disaster that befall a merchant whose capital is inadequate to the scale on which his imagination and ambition lead him to do business.

I suspect that the moment the distinctively educational function is strongly emphasized it will become evident that the college is nowadays educationally headless. The two officials nominally responsible for its direction lack time and scope. The President of the University is too busy and remote; his duties are executive, administrative, financial, representative. His interests and activities are necessarily less and less pedagogical; his contact with students, class-rooms, instructors, practically nil. The college dean, who takes his place, lacks pedagogical authority. His office has become increasingly clerical, hortatory and punitive. He is the keeper of the records, the interpreter of statistics, the chief probation officer. His intercourse with the individual student tends to be conditioned on the latter's delinquency. The boy who fulfils the minimum requirement is let alone. In any event, the dean's relations are with students only; over instructors or instruction, he has no real authority and no great influence. He is not appointed to the deanship by reason of pedagogical eminence. He is only a professor, detached for a while from his department because he happens to add executive ability and tact to the prevailing type of scholarship. The dean is not then fitted by the range of his acquirements or by distinctively pedagogical interest for the task of supervising the college organization and procedure. Either then the deanship must be reconstituted or a new office, say the principalship, be created. Not otherwise will the teaching function, as such, get adequate recognition. It certainly can get no such recognition from the department heads among whom it is now loosely scattered. These scholars and scientists are not going voluntarily to concede that the college interest is either distinct from, or prior to, or inconsistent with the interest of research. Left to themselves, as to a large extent they now are, they will continue to develop their departments in the research sense. They will proceed further on the theory that elementary teaching and special research "are both best done when done together," even when the teaching is literature, and the research philology or phonetics; that all new Ph.D's are *ipso facto* qualified to teach "what and as they think fit," during the period of incubation, when the university keeps them under observation to find out whether they will make good as investigators; finally, that the personal predilections of the scholars who constitute a department are bound automatically to provide just the courses that an undergraduate is in search of. Now, at every one of these points sharp emphasis of the college point of view will develop a conflict between the need of the boy and the procedure of the investigator. And for this reason: in the higher reaches of a fertile subject, where the investigator is busy, there are innumerable points of departure. It is practically immaterial where investigation begins; every trail leads somewhere. But at the lower level, that of the college boy, this is by no means the case. There, some things are more important than others; there, co-ordination within each subject, and between subjects that support and interpret each other, is indispensable, if the beginner is to achieve solid comprehension. Now this sort of thing does not take place automatically and incidentally, while the several instructors are pursuing their favorite scents. On the contrary, courses must be selected, mapped out, and conducted with the requirements of the student distinctly in mind.

The next move must be in the direction of reconstructing the preparatory school. As things now stand, the college is in fact the main hindrance to the vital, pedagogical treatment of the secondary period. External pressure has failed to make the preparatory school effective. A totally different conception must be introduced into the relations between the secondary school and the college. They must become continuous where now they fall apart. The motive on which the college vainly relies, self-realization, has got to be rendered operative at the earlier stage. As a matter of fact, the secondary period is far more favorable than the college to free exploration of the boy. In college, the proximity of the practical ends which loom up just ahead controls the situation. Imminent vocational or professional necessities should there largely determine both the content of the curriculum and the form of the instruction. In the secondary school, however, the material can be much more freely handled. It can be more readily derived from, less pedantically connected with, the boy's experience. Moreover the boy is himself more tractable. Early adolescence is a period of natural expansion, quick appreciation, ready responsiveness. It is preëminently the time for the liberation and recognition of the boy's power and purpose.

Reform of the preparatory school in this direction would require the transition to college to be less mechanically regulated. The examination system cannot be at once wiped out; but it can be gradually reconstituted. Entrance to college can, whenever the colleges so desire, be treated as a privilege. The range, seriousness and cohesiveness of previous study may be made the main factor in deciding to which of the excessive number of applicants further opportunity shall be extended. The College Entrance Board might readily be converted into an instrumentality for the ascertaining of these really vital facts.

Assuming now that the secondary school has actually laid bare the individual, has started up vital and characteristic activities, the college has something to build on. The elective system —for the time being I retain the name —becomes capable of intelligent application. The youth chooses; he selects or is effectively assisted to select his status. The college must then organize for him the intermediate steps to his chosen end. For this purpose it is worse than useless to maintain a diffuse and practically endless course of study. A compact, related and organized body of instruction in each of the fields which the college undertakes to cover, must be substituted for the *disjecta membra* of the present catalogue. Only in the very last stages can the undergraduate be credited with the knowledge necessary to a prudent choice between highly specialized alternatives. Seminary and research courses must be closed, not only to undergraduates, but to graduates, whose slender acquisitions require them still to repair to undergraduate classes. We shall thus have seen the last of two absurd phenomena now frequently observed: the undergraduate student, who, in default of thorough fundamental training, has prematurely escaped into a narrow research, which, whether worth doing or not, is not worth his doing then; and the mature graduate who takes part in an advanced seminary, while simultaneously making up fundamental deficiencies by attending elementary courses.

With the definite realization that the undergraduate comes to college in search of teaching in the pregnant sense of the word, other changes will take place. For example, the Freshman may there renew acquaintance with a teacher who won his spurs in a secondary school. Again, college teaching will do its painstaking piecework at the beginning of a new subject, instead of as now, only in the later and last stages, after wretched preliminary teaching, rather than demonstrated incapacity or uncongeniality has thinned out the ranks, and thus limited the size of the more advanced classes. The middleman, whether he be the changing assistant, detailed by the college, or the tutor hired by the boy, must be absolutely eliminated. The college professor will not only offer courses, but teach. I happen to know one, who, despite large classes, so construed his duty. His predecessor in the chair had lectured; unofficial quiz-masters did the rest at ten dollars per head. The new appointee declared war on the system; he frankly stated that he would put the knife into every examination paper that smacked of eleventh-hour cram. He proposed to do his own quizzing; twice weekly he would meet any students who cared to come for the purpose. The consternation of the first moments soon gave way to concurrent and energetic preparation. In time, practically every member of the class took part in the optional quiz. A genuine outburst of energy and productivity contrasted sharply with the previous sterility of the department. At the same time, the instructor in question was an original producer of distinction. He found that his teaching, once rationally organized, left him a respectable amount of time for his own researches.

Finally, emphasis of the teaching motive will put an end to commercialism. On this point plain speech is necessary. Efficient teaching is utterly irreconcilable with numerical and commercial standards of success. The colleges now want numbers; they must have and keep them, more or less regardless of quality. So elaborate are their equipments and appointments, so costly the maintenance of the plant,

that a temporary fluctuation in tuition
fees is a serious matter.[1] There arises
thus a spirited competition for students.
The various offices scrutinize the numbers of incoming classes as narrowly as
a merchant watches his daily sales.
They send out drummers who beat up
recruits and the credit man at home cannot be over-squeamish about accepting
and carrying business thus obtained.
This is the logic of the situation, from
which there is no escape. A high standard is incompatible with acute sensi-
tiveness to the reading of the trade

[1] "In spite of the great additions to the college's
invested property, it appears that at present a larger
proportion of its unrestricted income is derived from
tuition fees than formerly, and this means that *any
falling off in number of students* affects more di-
rectly the ability of the college to maintain its
necessary expenditure without harmful retrench-
ments." The University During the Last Twenty-
five Years," William Coolidge Lane, p. 5. (Italics
mine).

barometer. Nor can the college solicit on one basis and then exclude on another. It cannot put loyalty, tradition, athletics to the fore and then, when the clans gather, subject them to stringent tests of scholarly character. The college has thus tied its own hands. It cannot on existing lines effectively handle the students it has assembled; it cannot afford to apply methods or enforce standards that threaten the present enrolment.

So far, propositions that endeavor to face this problem have looked at it from the administrative or social side. Now the administrative problem may perhaps be solved by sub-dividing the over-grown college into several bodies, each in charge of its own dean; the social problem may be solved by housing the students in residential halls of the

Oxford type. But these devices do not touch the pedagogical problem: as long as all these sub-divisions merge without restriction as to total number in the lecture rooms and laboratories, contact between teacher and pupil is made impossible. The pedagogical problem is soluble only on the basis of a reasonably limited enrolment and the proffer of such courses only as the institution can afford to conduct without so far relying on fees that it must to a degree waive standards and ideals in order to get students. A comparatively simple calculation will discover how many students a college can, with its existing financial resources and laboratory facilities, teach; not admit and handle, but actually teach. It must admit no more. In selecting its material, it is then in position to go back of the mechanical examination returns, in order to ascertain whether the candidate is otherwise qualified to use the opportunities offered. How far beyond this point it can indulge the propensity for research, is something for subsequent consideration. Our output in the matter of investigation would indisputably increase in value and decrease in bulk, if the unflinching execution of the policy here urged should result in improving the efficiency of the colleges through lopping off entirely some of the graduate schools.[1] The college can be in

[1] It seems to me, for instance, that nothing is gained for research, and a good deal is lost for education, through the maintenance of graduate departments in colleges exclusively for women. Women are now admitted on equal terms with men to all graduate departments. The resources of our colleges for women are at best slender. Why should a considerable portion of them be taken away from the primary and unique object for which these colleges exist, in order to duplicate inadequately other opportunities that are already super-abundant?

close touch with the progress of knowledge without housing a graduate school
beneath its roof.

Thus far my suggestions are capable
of adoption without interference with
any college as a "going" concern. But
now I must point out that these suggestions do not exhaust our need and
opportunity. It is, therefore, pro-
foundly to be hoped that the reform
movement may be accelerated, guided
and carried further through independent demonstration outside the walls of
existing institutions. I submit that at
this juncture, increasing the resources
of our present schools and colleges so
as to enable them to do "more," does
not best serve the interests of American
education. Its urgent need is of institutions of different type; institutions
that, as over against the great educa-

tional factories, that meet the demand of the market, will embody the tentative enquiring spirit of the laboratory, where amidst simplified conditions, problems now glossed over may be attacked on their merits. Many such problems have been touched on in the course of these pages. The distractions due to expanding numbers and clashing ideals, have forced our hand in dealing with them. The situation has crystallized far too quickly; administrative necessity prevents it from now being completely broken up. Every institution has its recognized place in the elaborate and complicated system. The whole machine would be thrown out of gear by an experiment that, for example, undertook at once radically to readjust the present distribution of educational functions. It is nevertheless perfectly clear that this distribution is largely an historic accident; that a complete change of educational purpose has not yet found expression in the spirit, subject-matter, methods and organization of the curriculum. This is in the first place especially unfortunate, in respect to the secondary period. The secondary school is the key to the college position. On the vigor and intelligence of the secondary school, the permanent solution of college problems now depends. How can we decide the length, organization, content of a college course until we have in some sort mapped out, on the basis of successful experiment, the territory that can be covered in the secondary school? A splendid opportunity thus awaits a school outside the present system. Such an institution would furnish suggestions, models and standards to schools, not so circumstanced as to carry on educational experimentation. It would provide the college, the technical school, the professional schools with a scientifically determined point of departure; a definite basis upon which they could securely and intelligently proceed. There is no such basis now; nor within the established system can it be worked out in a scientific way.

THE END